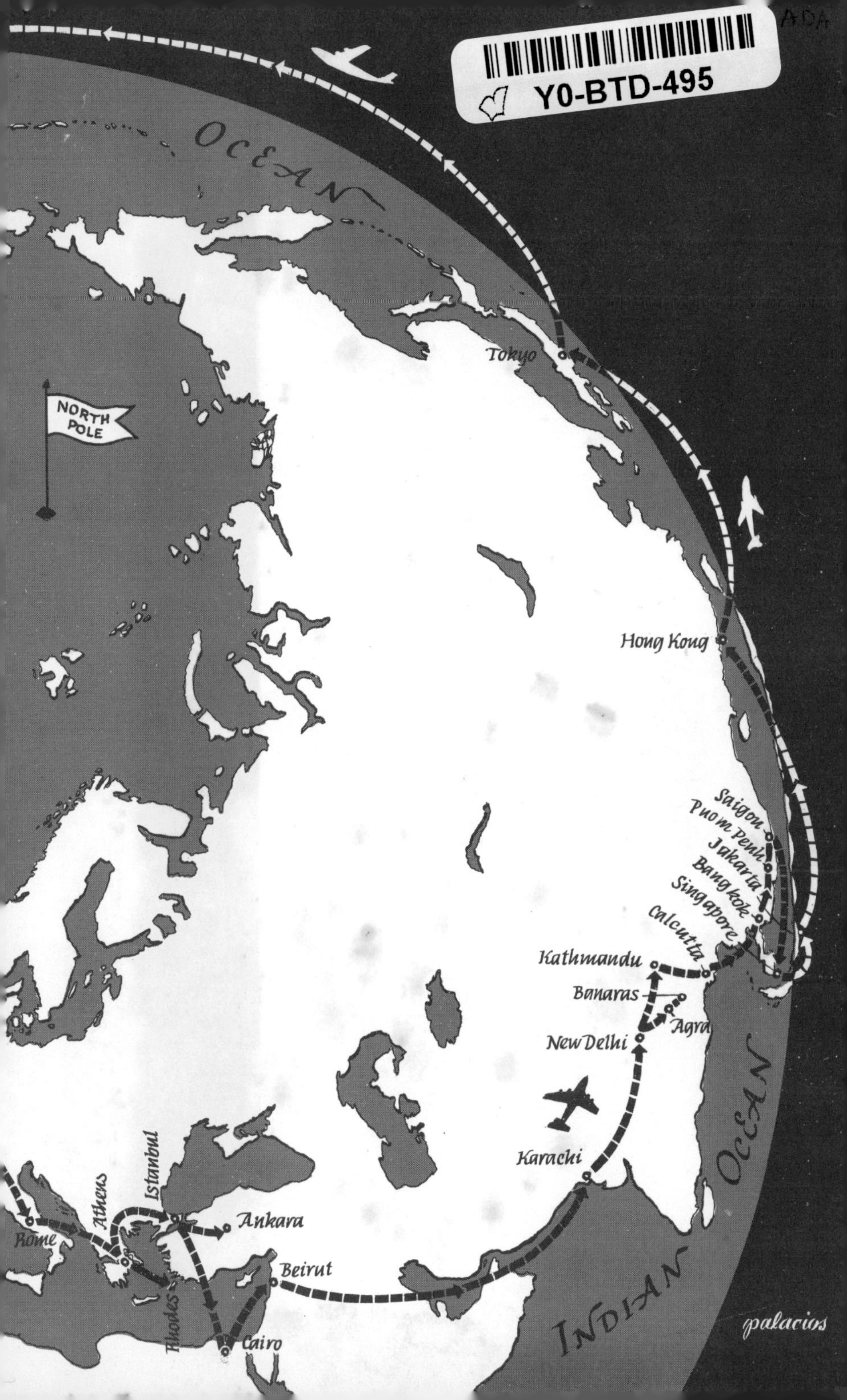

OCEAN

NORTH POLE

Tokyo

Hong Kong

Saigon

Puom Penh

Jakarta

Bangkok

Singapore

Calcutta

Kathmandu

Banaras

Agra

New Delhi

Karachi

Istanbul

Athens

Rome

Ankara

Beirut

Rhodes

Cairo

INDIAN OCEAN

palacios

DOORWAYS TO THE WORLD

Doorways to the World

REVEALING GLIMPSES OF PEOPLE AND PLACES IN WORD VIGNETTES AND PHOTOGRAPHS

By Elisa Daggs

DOUBLEDAY & COMPANY, INC., GARDEN CITY, N.Y.

LIBRARY OF CONGRESS CATALOG CARD NUMBER 60–9791

PRINTED IN THE UNITED STATES OF AMERICA

FIRST EDITION

ACKNOWLEDGMENTS

GRATEFUL acknowledgment is made to the many people around the world (some of whom became a part of the story), whose friendliness and guidance made this book possible.

In England — Mr. C. A. McIntyre, Deputy Press Officer of British Travel and Holiday Association; Mrs. Helen Hoskins; Miss Helen Lee. In Portugal — Mr. Antonio Nunes, Cultural Department Secretariat of Information. In Spain — Mr. José S. Eugene Ruiz, de la Direccion General del Turismo, Seville; Madame Paulette Toyo. In France — Mr. Jean-Michel Mettetal, Secretaire General du Tourisme Ile-de-France, Picardie; Madame Paul Morelle, Charge d'Accueil du Tourisme. In Italy — Capitano de Fregata Emanuele Cossetto, Chief of Press in the Office of the Prime Minister; Mr. Larry Howes, Press Attaché, American Embassy; Conte Fago-Golforelli; Mr. Conti Moretti; Mr. Corrado Lodi Focardi. In Greece — Mr. Nicholas Phocas, Secretary General of Greek Tourist Organization and Mr. Nicholas Velonis; Mrs. S. Andreadis, Director of "Their Majesties' Fund"; Mr. George Canellos; Madame A. Eliasco, Director of the Lyceum Club of Greek Women; Mrs. Lela D. Cassavetty. In Turkey — Mr. and Mrs. Munir Mudyyet

Bekman; Mr. Ferda Kocacimen; Mr. Memduh Tezel; Mr. Rüknettin Ulütug; Mr. Mubin Manyasig. In Egypt — Mr. Warren R. Broglie; Dr. Mohammed Zein-el Aberdeen. In Nepal — First Secretary of American Embassy, New Delhi, Mr. L. Douglas Heck; Dr. Shiva Mangal Singh Suman, Cultural and Press Attaché, Indian Embassy; Shail Kumar Upadhya; Mr. Ryszard Freleh. In India — The American Ambassador and Mrs. Bunker; Ambassador from the United Arab Republic, Mr. Omar Abou Richeh; Mr. Bernard Naylor Thorpe; Madame Komila Paranjoti; Mr. Tikki Oberoi; Mr. Humphrey Evans. In Thailand — Mr. Kormandi Thanutkid, Deputy Prime Minister; Madame Somchit Siddhighai, Acting Chief of the Thailand Tourist Bureau. In Cambodia — Mr. Kreng Nill, Head of the Press and Information, Ministry of Foreign Affairs. In Viet Nam — Mr. Opal, Director of the U.S.I.S.; Mr. Stafford Davis, Head of Press Department, U.S.I.S.; Mr. and Mrs. Bert Torrance; Mr. Sing Sheng; Captain Girvan H. Griffith. In Singapore — Mr. Herbert Shiro; the late Mrs. Fred Eu. In Hong Kong — Lonsco. In Japan — Mr. Edward Nickle, Deputy Public Affairs Officer, American Embassy; Mr. Kitamuri, Office of the Japanese Foreign Ministry; Mr. I. Yokota, Executive Director of Japan Tourist Association; Judge Yorihiro Naito; Mr. Yui Kittaka of Japan Air Lines; Mr. Yukio Watanaba; Mr. Ichiro Fujimura. In Hawaii — Mr. Richard Kimball; Mr. Karl Manke, Hawaiian Pineapple Co.; Mr. George J. Wimberly. And along the way — Mr. "Brick" Maxwell; Mr. Herbert F. Milley; Anthony (only man to see Pasternak) Brown; Miss Grace Dimelow; Mr. Otis Dozier; Mr. Stewart Parker Elliot, Jr.; Mr. Edward Carroll and Miss Helen Callahan; to Darby, Jessica, Anne, Maria, and Jack. And especially to Michael.

Contents

Doorways to the World

THE DOORS to the world are ajar for the traveler curious enough to touch the knob or blow upon the latch: doors carved of precious wood and inlaid with pearl; gilded and engraved and embedded with gems; doorways of gold, marble, and bronze. More beauty and riches, perhaps, have been lavished on doorways than on any other one thing of man's creation. Even the peasant's and the fisherman's doors are woven of straw, carved of wood, painted and hung with colorful cloth.

There are doorways for arrogant men that rise far above their heads, and doors through which man must stoop to enter, to teach him humility; doors through which he must crawl, to show penitence; and doors through which men can walk freely, as themselves.

And for the traveler who is adventurous enough to "fall out of line," doorways open at the turn of his head, leading, beyond the mysteries and treasures of ancient doors, to the people, who make the traveler no longer a stranger, and give meaning to a country's past.

It's what is happening now as well as thousands of years ago that gives the crumbling ruins their enchantment, measures their size and antiquity for the incredulous mind: incense burning in the ruined temples of Angkor, the sound of a flute floating from a black doorway in Calcutta.

There's not always time nor desire to see the world as a small boy on a hot, lazy afternoon watches a caterpillar on a fallen leaf, with his nose six inches above it. But sometimes. More often the fleeting glimpses through the doorways to the world are best.

Sometimes stories, whether fleetingly or lingeringly gathered, have no endings except those supplied by the imagination.

As twenty countries on four continents went by like telephone poles for four months, unfolding and disappearing below the wings of a Pan American 707 Jet and linking planes, the passing incidents, amazing places, people, and things were sometimes pieced together by the imagination, mortared with history and hearsay into stories with both beginnings and endings. Other impressions were fragments, of which everyday life is made—sometimes just the end, sometimes just the beginning. Sometimes it was like entering a theater in the middle of a scene and finding myself part of the incident.

These impressions, complete and fragmentary, along with the snap judgments and considered opinions of my camera, make up the vignettes in this book from twenty countries which I visited on an around-the-world flight from New York, across Europe, through the Middle East, Asia, the Orient, and back to California.

The people I met another traveler may never know, and some of the doorways photographed here *I* could not find again. Other travelers will meet other people, find other doors—perhaps many of the ones here. But these are my doorways to the world, through which I tasted the wine and shared the candle of people in unfamiliar countries.

The exact route I took around the world perhaps no one else may take. There are thousands of invisible lines across the vast oceans, deserts, above the towering mountains, traced by the routes of the jet clippers as they weave a web that snares the world for every man, translating miles into minutes . . . opening the doors to the world.

DOORWAY TO THE SKY

DOORWAY TO THE SKY

The Atlantic slid away swiftly under the arrow-shaped wings of the plane and the mosaic of gardens and fields of the British Isles took its place; later the spiderweb canals of Holland fleetingly spread out below; then the rocky coast of Portugal faded into the ocher hills of Spain, which quickly gave way to the pampered countryside of France and Italy; below the shining wings and powerful propellers lay a continuous land of counterpane. From the sky, a new dimension —boundaries drawn by the eye and peopled by the imagination—placid lakes, tossing seas, a castle on a mountain, villages, towers, minarets, pagodas, a white sail, a black freighter, an island meadow in the sea—the props of fantasy.

The sand lay in endless saffron waves across the Arabian desert. The sky was yellowed with sun. The heat clung like a thin yellow veil and wound around the legs of three travelers wandering across the sea of sand. A huge rock rose defiantly out of the distant sand ahead of them. To the burning eyes of the travelers, it may have seemed a cool desert castle, harboring a pool of clear water and deep shade. It seemed they struggled faster through the heavy sand, only to find the rock's sand-smoothed sides impenetrable, without a crevice in which to escape the heat. At the base of the rock lay a stingy black shadow where the three figures hovered until the shadow dwindled to a mere line as the sun reached the center of the sky, and then the three shadowy shapes moved wearily on.

A caravan far ahead, a lifetime away on the trackless desert, crawled through sand that had turned to orange, mixed with patches of black, and blown into plateaus. Here sharp red rock hills became masters of the sand wastes. Unwilling to give up the desert, the sand squeezed into every crevice and narrow valley between the rocks, in promising paths leading nowhere.

The hills and peaks stretched on for hundreds of miles, and

the long caravan appeared and disappeared among the boulders following a narrow sand valley that ran between the rocks for twisted miles, then branched off into a dozen trickling ends, one that might lead on—which? A dozen would lead nowhere. And who would know? Here the caravan came to a halt in a misshapen circle. Resting, motionless.

Now, far behind on the desert, only two figures struggled through the black sand and disappeared among the scorching rocks and appeared again, moving haltingly down a sand-drifted valley that was as lost as they—turning, twisting, going deeper into the hopeless caverns of rocks, more inescapable than the endless sand.

The twilight was turning the hollows of the rocks blue, and the last streaks of the flaming sun touched their tips and edges, transforming the whole great mass into a fiery black opal.

The two figures hesitated in the quickly darkening valley. They moved on, brushed against the narrow rock walls, stumbled, fell against the boulders in the suddenly icy night wind. . . .

But there were no three people lost in the desert; no caravan camping for the night for them to hope to reach. It was my eyes, the height, the desert, playing tricks on the willing imagination as the big clipper plane skimmed high above the Saudi Arabian rock and sand desert.

The lost travelers were the desert bramble that stirred in the wind and the tumbleweed that had broken away from its roots, rolling over the desert, tumbling over the dunes, moving up the valleys with the drifting sands. The camping caravan was sand-sculptured rocks that splayed over the desert in shapes to bewitch the mind, and the figures resting in the shadow of the rock castle were the drifts of sand.

But the burning sun that had flayed the silver wings of the plane all day was very real, and the sand, twisting in a million strings over the mountains of rock, lay below like the open brain of the world. The hours of very real, unconquerable space of furrowed sand growing dim in the fading light were bewilderingly true.

Night came like the closing of a shutter. The lights came on in the big 707 Jet. A buzz of conversation and laughter filled the plane, and a French novelist and his wife asked me to join them for an *apéritif*.

Soon the moon was turning the shining waters of the Gulf of Persia, below, into a field of drifting snow.

In the last six weeks and in the two months to come I was to discover the world behind the Doorway to the Sky, where the entr'actes of travel take place, aboard the big, round-the-world airliners: the only inhabited moving units in space known to man, which give his eyes possession of more of the world at one time than he can attain anywhere else short of the moon. A world filled with drama, humor, adventure. A private world in which to dream, or a place to know better other people from all points of the earth.

Over the Alps sixteen candles flickered on a birthday cake for a young Indian girl returning from school in Switzerland. Above the white isles of Greece, dotting the Aegean Sea, a couple quarreled an old sour quarrel. Over the plains of Anatolia an Egyptian actress traveling with a maid studied a new role.

A man and a girl met for the first time (but not the last) above the Mediterranean where the waters of the Suez and the Nile mix. The Parkinstons of Chattanooga won at bridge with the McGoldbernzes from New York along the coast of Jordan, and a turbaned Sikh worked at writing a cookbook. A child bravely permitted a tooth to be pulled high above Tel Aviv. Two men signed a long roll of contract that overran the little table and rolled into the softly carpeted aisle of the plane. An old man from Australia, a young girl from Minnesota, and a woman from California had met over the Marmara Sea and were seeing the world together. Other men and women found someone to *listen,* and discovered their own voices; found someone to *listen to,* and discovered they could hear.

Prompting the mind's fancy were a thousand sights—the sacred Ganges, coiled around the foothills of the Himalayas, which spiral upward in moiré terraces that cradle tiny temples and isolated houses bracing themselves along the furrowed fields propped against the mountainside; the blue Bay of Bengal suddenly disappearing and the tangled green jungles of Burma spreading a green, impenetrable blanket over villages, tigers, elephants, exotic flowers . . . and what else? nags the curiosity.

Above the China Sea on a fitful moonlit night, silver streaks of rain slid across the plane window and blew on into the night. The sky changed from black to white and, through the broken wall of foamy clouds, the silver plane headed straight into the moon. The clouds were white-feathered along the edges and rolled in billowing dark mountains on either side of the channel of moonlight.

As we passed through the fantasy of clouds over the mottled sea most of the lights in the plane switched off, and a little girl sitting next to me, who wasn't sleepy, confided quietly, "I'm going to get a Japanese doll in Japan, and——"

An old gentleman beside her, with a neat Vandyke, removed his eyeglasses, folded up the London *Times,* and introduced his granddaughter who, with this signal of coast-clear-to-talk, sat up straight and, in a hushed voice filled with intrigue, said, "Grandfather and I rode an elephant in—where was it, Grandfather?"

The old gentleman switched off his light and took the part of prompter in the background, "Siem Reap."

And on rushed the young voice, never repeating the words that were filled in by her grandfather, so that the story became, in the semidarkness, a strange mixture of the child's voice and the patient, amused voice of the old gentleman.

"And I flew a kite in—where, Grandfather?"

"Bangkok."

"And it was a girl kite and other children tried to catch my kite with theirs and pull it out of the sky, but they never did. They were boy kites. It's a game, and I have my kite—it's red and blue and striped and has eyes. I can run very fast and so can my kite. . . ."

Her eyes were wide and bright in the dim light.

"And Grandfather shot a—what was it, Grandfather?"

"A tiger."

"In—where was it?"

"Turkey, down near——"

"And he had a bath too."

"The tiger?" I asked. "No," she said, "Grandfather!"

"A Turkish bath," said the old gentleman with a snort, and continued, "You're right, my dear. I was beaten, scrubbed, rubbed, soaped, pounded, and thrown aside to dry."

The little girl chuckled with glee and said, "I had a real Siamese cat in Siam."

"In Thailand," corrected the old voice.

"How many kimonos will my dancing doll have on, Grandfather?"

"Seven, at least," replied the old man, "if she's a Takarazuka actress. Perhaps more if she's a geisha."

The little girl leaned back and sighed blissfully.

I switched off my light as the plane glided through the white night. True, I hadn't flown a kite in Bangkok, nor ridden an elephant in Siem Reap, nor shot a tiger, nor had a Turkish bath, and I might not get a Japanese doll, but I saw the world through other doorways.

A morning mist lingers in Hyde Park

England

TURN A CORNER: ANOTHER DOOR, ANOTHER LONDON

A LOVELY FOG was fitted into every seam and stretched around every corner of London; the vaporous mist was draped from tower to spire and joined neatly to each cornice, set into windows and carefully tucked into the doorways. It was not a heavy, gray-flannel fog tailored on Bond Street—it was a soft, sheer, chiffon fog, subtle enough to have been designed by the Queen's own dressmaker. It stirred like a soft, iridescent veil, with the old brownstones, green trees, and red bricks reflecting on it.

Through the mist, the flower boxes above the shop doors and in the window sills were soft, blurred prints of lavender hydrangeas, purple petunias, and pink geraniums. Wet cabs like giant black patent-leather slippers streaked through the streets and stood at the curbs.

Piccadilly Circus was a colorful, whirling merry-go-round of flower vendors, toughs, trams, and buses—noisy, pushing, bawdy, and blazing with neon struggling to get at you through the fog. St. James's Park was an enticing huge green cave under the heavy foliage of the trees, dripping with the spring drizzle, floored with the blunt, freshly cut grass, bristling with a dewy film. Mist muffled the footsteps on the pavement.

As it grew late, the blurred doorway lights of Soho's upstairs-downstairs lucky clubs and magic spots fell on the wet cobblestones and broke up into a confusion of reflections. The whole mass of London lights sifted through the foggy night from towers and roofs, windows, and signs. Lights strung along bridges floated in the Thames, marched along broad streets, flickered among the trees . . . and London twinkled like a bag of diamonds spilled through the fog.

Strangely London, supposedly a man's town, came to me in terms of fashion (the prerogative of Paris). But London has a quality very akin to fashion and, perhaps even more important, London has style.

There's style in the Trooping of the Colour; the "London season," a summer of gaiety and events from regattas to races, in which all London and its guests participate; the Mayfair doormen with their flowing mustaches and top hats;

the antique black cabs along Park Lane; the tulips; the green canvas chairs in Hyde Park; the stately homes (castles in any other language); the Chelsea flower show; Queen Mary's Rose Garden; Epsom Downs; even the big flat, black hats of the fish vendors of Billingsgate market; the cutaways at Ascot; the Beefeaters walking the guard at Tower of London, where the Crown Jewels repose. There's style in the flamboyant "Eliza Doolittles" hawking their flowers in Piccadilly Circus. There's style in the stuffy men's clubs and the stubborn domination of men over the affairs of London that gives the city the feminine charm of acquiescence.

There's style in the way the huge, busy city of London moves, dines, amuses itself; the way it politics and plays the game (whatever it is); and in its sophisticated acceptance of its own vast variations, which are the breath of fashion.

There's a saying, "If you don't like London's weather, wait a minute," and the cozy mist changes to clear, crisp, sunshine as quickly as the city shifts its scenery. If you don't like the look of London, "Just move along . . . turn a corner," where there's always another London—dozens of them. Move along to Cornhill, where the banks and financial buildings of "the City" (London's Wall Street) stand reverently around the Bank of England, affectionately known as the "Old Lady of Threadneedle Street." The coats of arms of the banks gleam in the sun: a golden grasshopper, a galloping horse, a gilded dragon, or an eagle. No skyscrapers or canyons—just money and quiet power.

There's the world of clubs and pubs, from White's ("Around the World in Eighty Days") to the Blackfriars, and thousands of workingmen's "locals"; the world of restaurants where London dines in London style at the Savoy grill; the Caprice back of the Ritz, thronged with the glamorous people in show business; at the Ivy off Cambridge Circus; on lamb chops at Scott's (declared superb by Clara Claasen); at Mitre Tavern on food fit for a Bishop, or at French, Chinese, Hungarian, Swedish, or Indian restaurants on cuisine from the world over.

There's Downing Street and Scotland Yard; the royal world of Buckingham Palace, the red coats of the guard

A world of pubs

Fog in a Soho doorway

flashing in the bright sun and their footsteps crunching on the gravel of the courtyard; Covent Garden; and the brilliant theatrical world of London, where over fifty shows play in one season at prices more like American movie prices; and the Sadler's Wells Ballet, so called because on the spot where the theater stands there was once a public music room conducted in 1683 by a Mr. Sadler, who discovered a well of sparkling clear water where travelers refreshed themselves: Sadler's Wells. Today, under the stage where Margot Fonteyn danced to fame, the well still bubbles.

"Around the corner," in the coffee houses of Chelsea, the pale-faced Bohemian ladies, in *skin*-tight pants, with shaggy Bardot hairdos, and the "Teddy boys" stare with fixed eyes into space over endless cups of coffee, expressing their contempt for the slightest natural emotion that might betray their state of being alive or in any way related to the despised human race—cold, restrained bohemians, so unlike their sloppy, slovenly, amateurishly "beat" counterparts in Greenwich Village.

London shifts the scenery: through Trafalgar Square—Berkeley Square—a Georgian doorway—Hyde Park—the Marble Arch—Westminster Abbey—Parliament. Along the gentle Thames, as busy as the rest of London with its barges and boats and bridges, London hurries, back and forth, busy, bustling, important, far-reaching, polite.

My cab, along with a stream of cars, switched off Park Lane into the circle before the door of the Dorchester Hotel into another London: Mayfair. Doormen moved from car to car in the endless line with umbrellas, delivering to the door the smartly-dressed-women-and-men-in-black-tie crowd. This hotel exuded personality and warmth, from the fabulous Oliver Messel suite on the roof—with its boundless view of flat, sprawling London, garnished with great clumps of park trees and the blue streamer of the Thames—down to the chef's special guest room three stories below the main floor (where I sampled vintage wines and caviar), and to my own small room overlooking a tulip terrace.

A note was in my room from the Marquis of Donegall, a friend for many years who was picking me up for lunch the next day. Already I was in love with many Londons.

The next morning the mist was waiting around the windows and hanging over Hyde Park. I took a short walk along the Park before getting a cab.

From the moment the London air touches your cheek, you feel—beyond the historical stone, efficiency, and movement—the dominance of the people of London over the city. The wide streets, though a solid mass that honks, scrambles, and squirms, seem to exist to take people where they want to go. The trees in the park are there to shelter Londoners from sun and rain, elevators in buildings are there to wait for them, restaurants to cater to them, and doors to be opened for them.

This is the great difference from New York, where I often feel, on returning after even a short absence, that New Yorkers are there merely to fill the streets, keep the revolving doors in motion, fill the elevators that must go up and down full, wait in line to occupy the seats of the theater, and hold down restaurant reservations siphoned off by irate headwaiters. It is difficult to explain why London seems made for Londoners instead of Londoners shaped for London, but it pleasantly does.

From the Dorchester roof—
flat, sprawling London

Perhaps it's the men in morning coats at the huge store of Fortnum & Mason who escort you to the cheese department; or the time taken at Harrods to help you purchase a package of tea as you would a bottle of French perfume, being urged to compare the bouquet of each tea. Or the theater with reserved seats not necessary to be picked up months ahead; the news hawkers who meet you halfway with the news (true or false); tea served everywhere at the magic hour, even to visiting sight-seers at Woburn Abbey, seat of the Duke of Bedford, and a hundred other little things.

The mist turned to drizzle as I took a cab to go to the Caledonian Market. The proud driver of the shiny black cab immediately started off with a long statement through a flowing mustache, not one word of which I understood. I

sat back in the seat in a state of shock and contemplated the driver; then I realized this strange language was cockney. It didn't seem possible that this man was speaking some form of the English language and that I couldn't understand it. I shuddered as I thought of twenty foreign countries to come. He waited for me as I hurried along the stalls of the market, staying under the little overhanging canvas tops out of the rain. The old silver and jewelry were tempting, and there was much food for imagination among the castoff glories of the many Englishmen who had lived for England in many parts of the world: old campaign buttons, sabers, and knives; uniforms, and relics of the "Poonah Poonah" life.

A lovely lavender Battersea box, a companion piece for one I prize dearly, caught my eye. I reached for it, but a

A broken bowl in Caledonian market

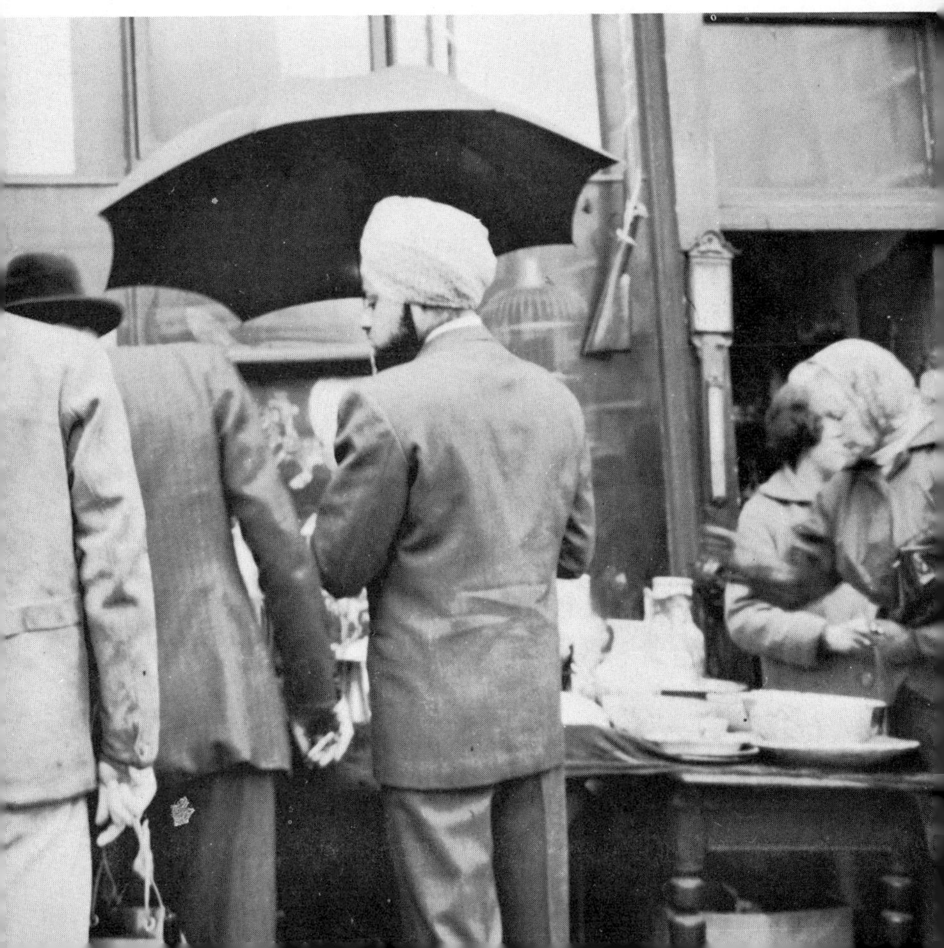

lovely Wedgwood bowl stopped me. As my fingers closed on one side of the frail rim, another hand securely grasped the other side, and the two hands lifted the bowl together. At the same time I realized I was standing under an umbrella and, as my eyes traced the arm away from the bowl, I found an extremely haughty British face looking at me. I let go of the bowl as the gentleman looked down his elegant British nose, but he gestured the bowl toward me and I again took hold of it. A look of disappointment filled his pale blue eyes, but he continued to hold the umbrella over my head. I offered the bowl back to him; he put his hand on the small blue-bordered bowl and I released it. So did he! And the fragile china crashed among the enameled boxes, bowls, and old silver pins. Without a word we each picked up a piece and looked accusingly at the other. He said, "My dear—my dear. . . ." I said, "Well. . . ." His pale eyes looked inquiringly at me as the rain poured on the big umbrella, which he adjusted over my head. The shopkeeper joined in the speechless argument with a shrug of his shoulders that ended with both hands suspended in the air, and he remained in this question-mark position with eyebrows lifted and lips pursed. A small crowd had been attracted by the breaking china; they stood looking from one to another of the three of us as if we were carrying on a heated argument and they were following the words from one face to another.

The shopkeeper dropped his arms with a crash, as if he'd completed a long, tiring speech. The gentleman with the umbrella looked at him, thrusting his thin neck forward and raising his eyebrows as if asking a question. The dealer picked up the fragments of the broken bowl one piece at a time, as if looking for the right pieces of a jigsaw puzzle, turned them over, and laid them crisply down in a pile. Bowing slightly, he took the small piece from my hand and turned it over, displaying a sticker with a price on it. I looked at the price and at the gentleman without a word. He handed the umbrella to me, took glasses from his inside pocket, adjusted them, and read from the small fragment held motionless in the dealer's hand. The crowd closed in. The gentleman replaced the glasses, took out a wallet, and handed a folded bank note to the proprietor, who quickly picked up the pieces, automatically whipped newspaper around them, and handed the package to the gentleman. He in turn handed the package to me, and I handed it back to the dealer, much as a hot potato would be passed along. The gentleman bowed and I nodded. He asked if I could manage without the umbrella, as he was dreadfully sorry but he must be going. The crowd looked disappointed and shuffled along, and I wandered through the crowded market, keeping my distance at the china tables.

Returning to the hotel, I told my cockney driver of the incident, and he made a long, profound (I'm sure) comment. Suddenly the mist was drawn back like a curtain and London stepped into a spotlight of brilliant sunshine. Birds sang in the parks, fruit stands threw back their canvases, and the world sparkled.

The following evening at a small dinner party at Lord Donegall's I heard some of his priceless jazz record collection, one of the greatest in England and America. Besides Donegall's broad interest in jazz music (for which he is sometimes called "Lord Jazz"), he is an enthusiastic member of the Baker Street Irregulars and editor of the *Sherlock Holmes Journal*. He introduced me later that evening to the world of Sherlock Holmes—another London. Since the club's founding in 1934, chapters have opened in Tokyo, Copenhagen, Toronto, New York, and more than forty other major cities in the States. The idea of the facetious Sherlock Holmes literary society stems from the eighteenth century when Horace Walpole satirized the idea that Bacon wrote Shakespeare. Similarly, in 1891 *Strand* magazine published an article theorizing that Dr. Watson wrote the Sherlock Holmes sagas. From this ridiculous premise Christopher Morley, Dorothy Sayers, and others formed the facetious literary club of the Baker Street Irregulars for the purpose of studying the abstruse points of, and exercising erudite discussions around, the famous Sherlock Holmes detective stories by Sir Arthur Conan Doyle. The club names are taken from the titles of the dozens detective stories, such as "The Speckled Band," "Six Napoleons," and "The Dancing Men," and "The Five Orange Pips."

London was in a rainy mood and narrow Northumberland Street was streaked with misty light reflected on the wet cobblestones. At the end of the street dim lights showed through the square windowpanes of the Whitbread Sherlock Holmes Inn (or Pub). London, like all England, is filled with dedicated inns. It is said the British erect statues to those whom they admire or esteem, but inn signs are reserved for those whom they honor and love. This is an honor particularly appropriate for Holmes, since Sir Arthur Conan Doyle endowed this famous character of fiction with maternal French ancestors who loved food. Certainly, Holmes "lived" in the still-famous Frascati's in Oxford Street, frequented Goldini's, and Watson spent many a day in the Criterion Bar.

Lord Donegall's guests sat at a table along one side of the pub. Upstairs was housed a collection of Holmesiana, one room a replica of 221B Baker Street as it would have appeared in 1897, complete with scrapbook, unanswered correspondence still transfixed to the mantelpiece by a jackknife, tobacco stored in the Persian slipper, and the Inverness cape and deerstalker hat hanging on a peg by the door. This room was displayed in New York in 1952, with a sound record of street noises that would have been heard along Baker Street at that time.

We settled down to talk about Holmes, the Baker Street Irregulars, and the improbable afterlife of Sir Arthur Conan Doyle, who was a great student of metaphysics and was intent on contact in his afterlife with the world he had left, which has led to many experiments by spiritualistic mediums to attempt communication with him (and later led me to 9 Curzon Street and to one of London's favorite clairvoyants). It was a perfect night to dwell on the daring escapades of the world's greatest detective, from whom all "private eye" sagas have sprung. The rain slanted across the windowpanes and through the door into the dimly lighted, cozy room came people in raincoats with turned-up collars, carrying dripping umbrellas—people who, within the context of the pub, might well have been Watson arriving for a rendezvous with Holmes; or Holmes himself, famous for his inexhaustible disguises as a Tibetan lama, a plumber, a bookseller, a

Rainy rendezvous with Sherlock Holmes

French workingman, showing up disguised as a Londoner.

The walls were covered with original illustrations from the famous stories and photographs of the period.

Contrary to popular opinion, there is excellent food in London, I found as we moved on later to Charco, a tiny restaurant in Bray Place, Chelsea, the restaurant of Lord Vivian, who is personally responsible for its décor, its excellent food, flowers, and every detail. Needless to say, reservations must be made in advance.

It was late when we left Charco, and the rain had cleared. London night life was moving toward the West End. The moon was floating among scudding clouds, and Westminster Abbey was casting beautiful black shadows of its towers. Buckingham Palace was patterned with the shadows of scurrying, puffy clouds; moonlight fell through the open patches in the trees in Hyde Park; the rows of chairs were in perfect order along the tulip beds. London was suddenly as fresh and clear-eyed as the English countryside, which is a thousand other Englands to come back to some other time, since I was leaving the next day for Amsterdam and on—for four months around the world.

Holland

THE UPSIDE-DOWN DOORWAYS

REFLECTED in a canal in Amsterdam, the upside-down doorway of a terraced and gabled house ripples in the water; a duck skims through the reflected doorway, and fish swim in and out of its white-outlined windows. The reflection is as real as the house upon the street.

The canals that are woven over Amsterdam like a spider's web turn the parked cars along the banks upside-down in the water. The overhanging trees, the hundreds of arched bridges, slim patrician houses, and the back doors of shops all become Siamese twins, with their reflections as vivid as they. Droves of bicycles that race along the streets bordering the canals on both sides perform this same feat upside down in the water.

Many of the little town houses along the Voorburgwal and other main canals have become commercial buildings, though they still keep their lace curtains in the door panes, the beautiful paneled wooden doors polished, and the brass and ironwork shining.

The canals run in widening semicircles, crossed with *grachten* (small connecting canals) that spread out from the harbor like a spiderweb cut in half, and are used for sightseeing boats, commercial barges that poke through the water with coal and sand, and for mooring the hundreds of houseboats that have taken over whole canals. Modernly furnished and with potted geraniums on their porches and sun decks on their tops, the houseboats make homes for thousands of Holland's overflow population. The canals are used not at all for daily transportation.

The only means of traversing the sun- and shade-dappled waterways is by the big modern sightseeing boats (water buses) that, once on their scheduled route, make no stops. The riders are captive until the water bus runs its course. The voice of a guide giving continuous, memorized tourist data in French, English, and Dutch echoes into a loudspeaker; the big, cumbersome boat backs up occasionally to get around a corner of a narrow canal. Little canals slip by, shady and mysterious. The reflection of a bridge or flowers or a café sparkles enticingly down another way, but the big bus-boat booms along with its loudspeaker blaring, just like a bus on a highway. There are no gondolas, no taxi boats, no boats for hire to drift into little side canals off the beaten path.

Though Amsterdam once lay proud claim to the title "Venice of the North," the romance of the canals has been lost. Though the people of Holland have become too occupied with rush and growing and efficiency to keep the canals alive, it seems Nature and the architectural beauties of Amsterdam cater to the canals as if to play them up. The flower markets at their walls throw masses of reflected color into the water; the cafés built along the banks put on gay table covers and the garden terrace of the Amstel Hotel edges the water with potted plants; the parks grow green to their edges and trees lend their green leaves and branches for decoration, as every day the canals paint on their mirrored surfaces the panorama of the city along their banks.

Tulips cover the city in patches of color, like huge, pink, yellow, white, red, and black scarves dropped here and there. The Rijksmuseum door opens onto a small park that's a riot of colorful tulips iridescent in the yellow sunlight, and behind its doors are the great, somber paintings of Rembrandt: The Night Watch, which is almost *too* restored, and The Directors of the Cloth Makers' Guild. And, in my opinion the greatest of all, Prayer Without End, by Nicolaes Maes. But Rembrandt's soul-searching self-portraits hang in the Mauritshuis in the Hague, along with Vermeer's View of Delft and Young Girl with Turban.

Behind the simple doors of a small white town house, the famous Dutch diamond house of Streep has rows of men with telescopic eyes cutting piles of diamonds into more "best friends for girls."

Flowers are always formed into planned gardens in Amsterdam, but through the farm lands, where houses with deep-pointed roofs rise like pyramids out of the green desert, the beauty of the countryside depends on the canals, the trees, and the little dooryard gardens.

Trees mirrored in the Voorburgwal

Houseboats on the canal

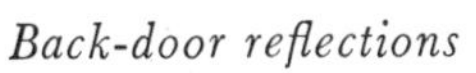

Back-door reflections

Seeing Amsterdam the easy way

At each city door,
a bicycle

On each country doorstep,
wooden shoes

As there is in Amsterdam at least one bicycle in front of almost every doorway, there are on every farmhouse doorstep wooden shoes—big, little, and middle-sized. As the Japanese step out of their wooden clogs at the door onto their grass mats in their one-toed tabis, the Hollander leaves his wooden shoes at the door and wears his heavy woolen socks or soft slippers.

A typical wooden door, paneled and weather-scarred, opens into the simple home of a Dutch farmer, housing his family and sheltering his stock, for the pyramid farmhouses are both house and barn under the same roof. The four-sided deep roof is a loft filled with sweet-smelling hay. In the center of the house is a square court below the opening into the loft where grain, straw, farm implements and other necessities are kept.

Around this center room, the house occupies half of the one-story space and the barn the other half. A small door at the back of the house (or barn) opens into the stable and stalls for the horses and cows . . . this part does not smell like new-mown hay—it smells like a barn.

114
MODE-IN
DAMES
HARTI

Hay in the loft, cows in the back room

Weighing in the cheese

The house is clean and neat, with rag rugs spread on the polished floors, and simple furniture. There is fresh lace at the little windows and flowers along the front of the house, which gives no evidence of its close proximity to the animals under the same roof. Holland farmers have lived this way for centuries.

All country roads around Amsterdam lead to the Alkmaar cheese market, where the big, red-painted balls of cheese are sold every day from spring to fall. The cheese carriers, in white suits and wearing large colored straw sailor hats, take the cheese on sled-like wooden carts, with a strap on their shoulders, to the town weighing machine, the *wagebouw,* in a building with painted medallions on the facade and a carillon in the tower.

In this tiny country, it is not far to anyplace, and the fishing village of Volendam nearby clings to the flat coast along the green inland sea. Big brackish-red boats with black nets hanging from their masts unload their fish along the one main street that perches on the dike that follows the sea. The men swagger gregariously about the boats in their full pantaloons of heavy black wool and short fitted jackets, black scarves, and fur hats. Their wooden shoes click along the stone street. They are very handsome, and these heavy woolen clothes and fur hats are very costly.

There are no women around the boats, but a few on the streets, with their starched-lace cornucopia hats, and multistriped aprons over Quaker-like dresses. The minute Volendam fishermen's houses are snuggled down in back of the dike and its row of shops that edge the street.

Pantaloons in Volendam

Fishing boats along the dyke

Lace-curtained lookout

The doors, painted red, green, and white, have little curtained lookouts, smaller than a face; a knock at the door is answered through this. The name of the owner is printed on the door plaque.

There's a sadness hanging over the fishing village of Volendam like a faint mist from the sea, for the diking up and poldering of the Zuider Zee cuts Volendam off from the live sea, and the fishermen are slowly drifting away into factories. With the sea shut off, the village will finally cease to be a fishing village.

Holland is changing the actual geography of its country. By diking the Zuider Zee, it gains an expanse of much-needed land to keep up with the rapidly increasing population. Land that is now being wrested from the sea, but still lies below sea level, will house thousands of people.

Holland's great castles, with their heavy round and square towers, are truly like fortresses that rise strangely out of the flat land. Vine-covered Muiderslot Castle rises like a phantom from the grass along a little river.

Acres of tulips

Outside Amsterdam, the Garden of Linnaeushof is built around the original botanical workshop of Linnaeu, the flower genius of Sweden who came to Linnaeushof two hundred and fifty years ago. Not only the biggest, the brightest, the blackest, the whitest tulips in the world grow here, exquisitely arranged, but the garden is a masterpiece of landscaping—with flowers, trees, shrubs, arbored paths, and water. Around the wooded garden grow fields of tulips and hyacinths to make bulbs to send to the world's Park Avenues.

Inside the door of a little shed in the center of acres and acres of tulips and hyacinths are the spades, forks, wheelbarrows, tools, and baskets of tulip bulbs that the men in the gardens of Linnaeushof use to turn the parks into a sea of tulips in spring. The door is reflected in a grass-fringed canal that brings water to the thousands of plants and the pools and streams of the beautiful gardens.

Portugal

THE LONELY DOOR OF NAZARÉ

BY DAY, this doorway is like any other doorway in the small fishing village of Nazaré on the coast of Portugal, with the sun bleaching the clothes flapping in the tireless wind. But when the sun is lowering and the last dripping boat is safely on the beach and the brown nets spread upon the still-warm sand, this doorway is different from the other doors.

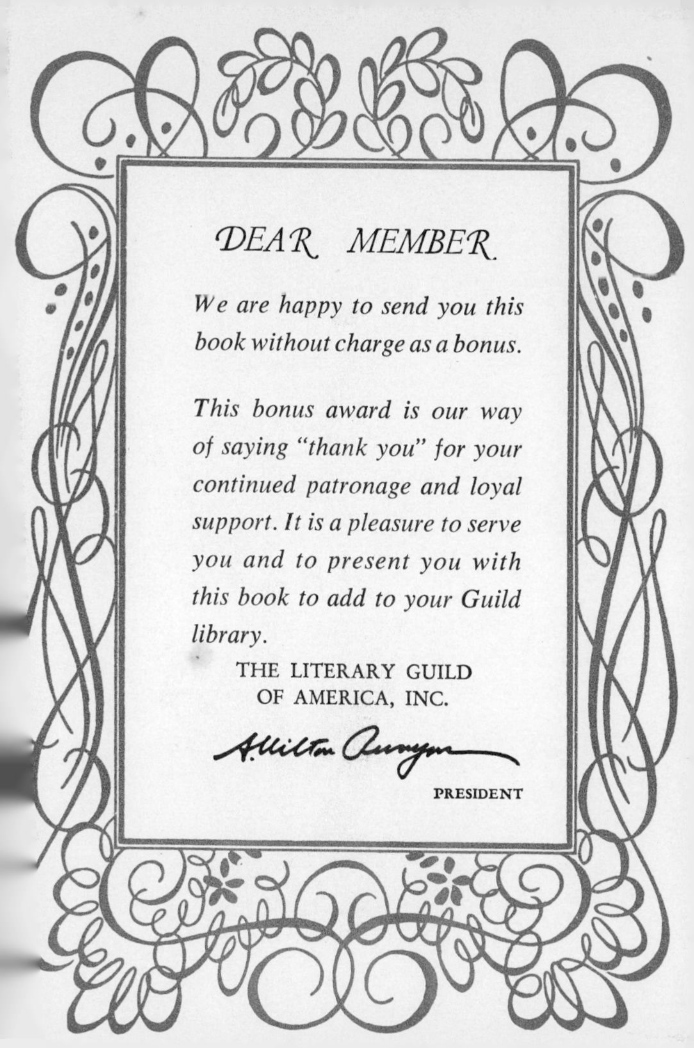

DEAR MEMBER

We are happy to send you this book without charge as a bonus.

This bonus award is our way of saying "thank you" for your continued patronage and loyal support. It is a pleasure to serve you and to present you with this book to add to your Guild library.

THE LITERARY GUILD
OF AMERICA, INC.

PRESIDENT

The weather-bleached house with the faded blue door crowned with the iron balcony of an attic window is like hundreds of other fishermen's houses that follow the golden crescent of sand until it ends in the shadow of the mountainous cliff that turns out to sea.

Thin twists of sand scuttle around the doorway of the little house and slip over the stone floor. Inside, it's cool and dark. Two straight chairs face a round table in the center of one of the two small rooms, and an oil lamp sits in the center of the blue cloth edged in coarse lace. Blue and white pottery bowls are stacked on a shelf over a charcoal stove.

From the doorway a young girl steps quickly into the street with a baby wrapped in her long black cape, drawn tight against the wind. She walks the narrow street that holds the sand and the houses apart.

Now the little house is empty, as are all the houses of Nazaré at sundown when the fishing boats return, piled high with glistening fish, the pigskin wine casks empty.

The anxious faces of the other women of Nazaré along the sea wall are turned to the sea, but the young girl's thin face is determined as she looks always away to the cliff or the

. . . like large black birds

houses. The black cape blows against her bare legs as she walks the length of the houses, back and forth. The fishermen's wives perch on the stone streets along the wind-sheltered houses and on the sand like big black birds, with their capes covering their heads and spread over their bare feet. They watch the sea as if for the first time, but every day for a lifetime they have sat on the sand as the sun faded, straining for a glimpse of a bobbing boat in the green distance. They wait motionless and melancholy for the return of husbands, sons, fathers, brothers, and sweethearts.

Many men of Nazaré do not return from the sea, and the law of Nazaré forbids the fisherman's widow to remarry.

Every day the excitement of the returning fleet sets the sands in motion. Men with ropes and oxen crunch through the sand to pull the first boat ashore. Children run to the edge of the sand; women hover in groups, holding small children who strain to take part in the activity. A child breaks away and runs to his father, who hoists him by one arm into the boat to take the short ride on the sand as the oxen heave and pull. The huge waves are pushing the boats in fast, and the men work frantically to keep them from piling up. Another boat hits the sand and a dozen men cling to the brown serpentine rope as they drag the boat out of reach of the tide.

The woman with her baby is alone in the street. Her eyes gleam with resentment against the sea as the heedless waves pitch the boats upon the sand, bringing other women's men back to them.

Women watch and talk among themselves and men shout and tussle with the brown nets as they spill the silver stream of fish into big wooden bowls and flat baskets—silver slivers of sardines; shining, tumbling, squirming baby eels; huge slabs of iridescent fish; streamers of polished swordfish and long patent-leather eels flip out of the nets. The fishermen arrange and rearrange the fish in the bowls with pride, and hoist them upon the sea wall for those who bid, bargain, and buy.

The light is fading as the hungry waves lick at the sun. The dusk turns the little blue door of the widow of Nazaré into a hollow shadow and the white walls to gray.

Boats bobbing in the green distance

Now the house betrays its sorrow as the fishermen swagger through the streets in tartan shirts, heavy black pants and oilskins, with their wool stocking caps flipping about as their children cling to their arms and their wives follow them silently to their little cottages . . . now the door of the little house is different from most doors in Nazaré.

The sweet, salty clothes and the cage with its small golden birds have been taken inside. But there are no shining oars, dripping with the sea, propped beside the doorway; no yellow oilskins, smelling of the boats, hanging on the line. No shiny black oilskin water bags swing from the balcony. There is no crack of light tracing the doorway, nor the smell of fresh fish on the charcoal. There are many widows in Nazaré, but never one so young and bitter. Every day she climbs to the top of the cliff, with eyes avoiding the sea that dimples and plays in the morning sun.

Here more fishermen's houses perch around a tiny chapel with a blue and white porcelain tile roof. In the minute chapel the old black wood is polished and the altar scorched to charcoal where the candles have burned out for centuries. The walls of porcelain and the fresh white altar linen gleam in the candlelight. A tiny window looks out on Nazaré far below along the curve of the sea, where the houses crowd as close as possible to the sea wall and the black boats, decorated in red, blue, and yellow, rest upon the sand. Some boats have the all-seeing eye painted on either side of the high Phoenician prows that cut through the mountainous breakers, too often hiding a deadly shoal.

There are always boats left on the beach with men asleep in their shadows, sheltered from the sun and the wind. All day every day old men sit on the sands and mend nets or tie new ones. Sober-faced little boys play among the boats. Little girls sit on the sand like pouter pigeons in their seven pleated petticoats, crocheting endless yards of lace to edge more petticoats. Young women whose lovers are at sea hum a mournful *fado* as they go about their work.

Little shops line the cobblestone square. A flower garden of blue, green, and yellow pottery clusters around a shop door, but life in Nazaré is lived on the flat sandy beach.

Someday the young widow of Nazaré may look again at the sea. But one day she may grow hopeless and disappear, or return to the home of her mother's people, who farmed

Flower garden of pottery

the lowlands in Ribatejo along the Tagus—people who, according to her mother's tales, turned to fishing when the floods came too often to the *mouchões*. There on the fertile swamplands on the banks of the Tagus the river fishermen and the farmers are half seafarers, half land-dwellers, all living at the mercy of the river.

The ancestors of the Nazaré widow grew weary and rebellious at returning to the mud-soaked cabins to start again. Restlessly the swamp farmers looked to the fertile lowlands and pastures stretching toward Spain, where the grain fields of Portugal wave on the broad plains of Alentejo. They longed for the high hills of sunshine beyond, with orange groves and clean, dry forests of cork oaks to shelter them, but, hopelessly, they drifted, generation after generation, among the fishermen along the coast of Portugal.

Many nights inside the little house of Nazaré the young widow dreams of this land away from the treacherous black sea, a land beside the sea of golden grain rippling in the wind, a sea you could trust, where a man could swing a sickle in the sun and return safely home at dusk.

She hates the silver stream that pours from the nets of the Nazaré fishermen and runs like a silver ribbon through the life of Portugal, tying the quiet, melancholy people to the sea. Not only those who live within the sound of the sea, but those who look upon its endlessness from the hills and cities of Oporto and Lisbon; the peasants from the wine lands that have made Portugal famous; people from the cork-oak forest that supply cork to the world; the herdsmen from the plains and pastures that produce the cattle and the fighting bulls—all are tied to the sea.

Big, modern Lisbon, rebuilt after the earthquake, has the sea at its feet. The old town, Alfama, rises from the waterfront, a colorful fishing village in the heart of Lisbon. Red sailboats drift into the harbor as fishermen return to the cottages that cling to the narrow, perpendicular, tangled streets. A colorful mixture of houses, shops, baskets of fish; children, cats, vegetables; little doors with glass lookouts; old churches, mountains of steps, and miles of cobblestone fit into the mosaic puzzle of Alfama.

In the big Lisbon market behind the Cais do Sodré, the

Gothic Lisbon

fish auction arouses Lisbon at six. But not until midmorning is this night-owl city really awake and stirring.

Hours later, commuters from elegant Estoril pour into the Cais do Sodré from the first-class compartments of the little trains that amble along the seaside with their doors wide open, stopping at posh little suburbs for the Lisbon-bound.

By this time the auctioneer, who starts the fish at a high

price which he lowers until he gets a bid, has barked his last mumbo jumbo for the day. The uninhibited fishwives (*varinas*), who sometimes come to tussles over a big silver fish, have shouted, shrieked, and filled their baskets with the very best fish for the fewest escudos.

And these legendary *varinas* are far away in the busy streets of Lisbon with their flat baskets of dripping fish on their heads; weaving among the trams, two-story buses, and shiny cars, they become part of the Lisbon scene. Their gold earrings flash under the dripping fringe of fishtails, and their colorful skirts and aprons flip about as they lustily sing out the old story, "Fish for sale!"

The same sea that lashes the beach at Nazaré, lingers in the harbor of Lisbon, and laps the sands at Estoril, has for centuries brought riches of all kinds to Portugal, this small strip of land cut off from Europe on one side by mountainous Spain and connected with the world on the other side by the Atlantic.

Portuguese seafarers, explorers, crusaders, and conquerors went forth to return rulers of countries in Africa, South America, and unknown lands. Portugal's seafarers were first to round the Cape of Good Hope and to reach India by sea; first to land in China, Japan, and Australia. And Magellan's famous sail around the world in 1519, taking over three years, was the crowning Portuguese victory over the sea. Today a Pan American Jet Clipper could cover Magellan's route, circling the world, in less than thirty-eight hours.

Ornate Masteiro dos Gerónimos

Between the casino and the sea

Out of sight and sound of the sea, north across the Tagus, far from the wheat fields for which the widow of Nazaré longs, are the barren hills and slopes of Douro. Nothing grows on these stingy hills except the grapevines that crawl over the land that is more rock than soil, feeding on the cracked clay, drinking in the torrid sun. So high and rugged is the terrain where the grapes ripen red, close to the sun, that the fragrant baskets are brought down the plunging Douro River in flat *rabelos* tossing over the rapids and dodging the rocks. And, as for centuries, the grapes are pressed by singing peasants half intoxicated with the bouquet rising from the grapes beneath their feet.

The rich port wine that ages in the dark caves dug in the chalk hills is the miracle of the vines brought by Count Henrique from Burgundy eight hundred years ago. From these vines, tenderly nourished by the Portuguese, came port wine, to travel to the ends of the world to be relished by the rich and the rare. These same elegant internationals now come to Portugal, to nearby Estoril, to gambol on the beach and to gamble in the red casino.

Between the two lies an esplanade woven of lush green grass, trailing vines, fountains, and clipped hedges, laced

No one left to sn

with gravel paths dotted with scarlet geraniums, and bordered with palm trees, sloping from the red-canvas-enclosed terrace of the casino to the platinum sands of Estoril Beach like a rich oriental rug rolled out for the titled and for the solid-gold millionaires from far and near; for the fabulous parade of maharajas, dukes and duchesses, ex-kings and future queens, princesses, enfantas, countesses, and barons, as they shift from the dripping sea to the casino, dripping with diamonds and emeralds, wrapped in chinchilla and weighted with bank notes. The elegant Estoril Palace Hotel facing the esplanade pampers them with cocktails, fine wines, and delicious cuisine.

All of the games in Estoril are expensive and must be played by the rules—no stripping to bikinis to swim in the Dior-blue water, but money can be shed by anyone with passport in hand, at the roulette tables in the shabby back room of the casino, down to an absolutely nude bankbook.

In the cabañas clustered on the beach, it might very well be imagined, these dilettantes loll, proofreading the latest edition of *Almanach de Gotha*. Touted to be the playground of kings, here there can scarcely be anyone left to snub, and a name dropped here—is dropped!

In Estoril's abridged dictionary, *Windsor* is a castle in England; *Knickerbocker* is singular for plus-fours; *Christians* are people who are Baptists, Episcopalians, Protestants, and Catholic (as are all the Portuguese); and *Parsons* is plural for preacher. *Sinatra* is undoubtedly Sintra misspelled; *Parker* is a fountain pen; *Oberoi* a chic hotel in India; *Liz* is the Queen of England; *Bardot* is a typographical error that appears often in print all over the world; and *who* is Elsa Maxwell?

Those who come to Estoril rarely leave the environs of the esplanade, the snobbish hotels that hover around it, and the beautiful homes among the palms and geraniums.

But some of the splendor of Estoril overflows onto the soft-focus fishing village of Cascais, surrounding it with beautiful royal-exile mansions, hotels, and red geranium gardens. The narrow streets hide famous intimate restaurants among the boatmakers' shops, lace-curtained houses, and taverns. Every doorway has a cat, aloof and indolent.

In every doorway a cat

The fountains of Queluz still sparkle

Estoril pales beside the fabulous playgrounds that have marked Portugal's three dynasties of the past. The fountains of Queluz that still sparkle around lapus lazuli figures, the clipped spinde trees and box hedges set off the pink palace like a pale rose, patterned after the French so perfectly that to step inside its garden is to leave Portugal.

The paths of Queluz were familiar to the footsteps of the rich and the famous from all of Europe. The sentinel, bare-bosomed sphinxes still stand, heavy with lichens, at the garden gate, guarding the exquisite furnishings of the palace. Its art treasures and paintings were the background for a life that was as gay and rich as any in all Europe.

Gothic, Moorish,
Manuelin, pseudo . . .

. . . heavy with lichens

From the balustrade—the valley and the sea

Lord Byron felt akin to the romance of Sintra when he came to Portugal to stay long and contentedly. The glitter of riches from New World discoveries, piled high in Portugal, brought the world to its doors. Sintra, one of the few fairy-tale castles left in the world, towers high on a wooded pinnacle, surrounded with pines, palms, waterfalls, and masses of red and pink camellias, clouds of wisteria, and a carpet of dewy ferns. It is mysterious and was once virtually inaccessible. The mist drifts over the ravines and around the turrets. The air is heavy with the fragrance of woods and moss. There's always another flight of worn stone stairs leading to a balustrade that overlooks the valley and the sea.

The Castle of Sintra,
a part of every king's life

For centuries, since the reign of John of Aviz, the Castle of Sintra has been a part of every king's life, and each has left his mark on the old castle, which grew more beautiful despite the bastard appendages of Gothic, Moorish, Manuelin, and pseudo-Victorian Gothic.

Its romantic tower imprisoned Alfonso VI for six years while his scheming brother sat on his throne and made love to his wife.

The Portuguese are said to get their courtesy from God, their manners from the French, and their melancholy from the sea, but their fierce, steadfast devotion to those they love was born in the heart of the first Portuguese . . . In the immortal love story of Pedro the Burgundian Prince and Ines de Castro, who was killed because she was Castilian, Prince Pedro avenged the death of his love by hunting down her destroyers and tearing their hearts out. Alcobaca Monastery cloistered Ines and her lover, who came to lie beside her years later so that on Judgment Day, when he arose, he would look first upon her face.

But the young widow of Nazaré is sentenced by the sea to wait alone. In time, when she has made peace with the relentless waves and her son is old enough to match his strength with the ropes and the nets, she will sit upon the sands of Nazaré at sundown and challenge the forgetful sea. The men of Nazaré battle the sea with their hands—the women of Nazaré fight the sea with their hearts.

. . . and the sea

A woman of Nazaré

Spain

DOOR OF THE MATADOR'S JEWEL BOX

LIKE a fabulous jewel in a box, the matador's bolero sparkles and glows in the little fitting room of the tailor of Seville.

The scarlet curtains have been drawn aside and the door to the fitting room propped back with the embroidery board that now is empty of its proud, arduous work.

Unshaded, the raw light from the ceiling picks up every glint of the 24-carat-gold and silver embroidery that has been threaded into the pale blue satin, a stitch at a time. Trading reflections, the light rays and the embroidery surround the chair with a veritable mist of mica. The glittering pants lie across the chair with their white muslin cover turned back, like a bed in a fine hotel waiting for its expected occupant to step in.

With the long basting threads still tracing the hem, the matador's pink cape billows from the peg on the mirror which will unfold, threefold, to reveal the beauty and perfection of the costume as the matador turns and twists. The red-flowered carpet has paled beside the splendor of the gold and the brilliance of the cloak.

The tailor shop, so well known to the famous names plastered on the billboards announcing the *corridas* in Madrid and Seville, would go unnoticed by the passerby among the other shops on the cobblestone street in the shadow of the Giralda Tower of the Cathedral of Seville. In front of the fitting room and overlooking the narrow street is another room, with the glaring sun reflecting into the windows by which the young girls embroider the gold and silver patterns on the boleros. The great bullfighters—Manolete, Dominguín, Ortega, Pedres, and others—for years have selected embroidery patterns and satins from the little tailor of Seville. Now "The Yank," the young torero from "The States," comes with the Spanish matadors and picadors through the streets with crowds at their heels.

What matador will come today? Which will drop the red curtains and array himself in the finery laid out so carefully, while the whole shop seems to hold its breath as the little tailor hovers around, patting and smoothing.

The young embroidery apprentices string gold threads across the tailor's shop. One girl cranks the rickety spinning wheel while the other holds the spidery threads that twist through her fingers into one strong embroidery thread.

Another pink cape, half-cut, falls over the side of a table in the center of the big room off the fitting room, which is so dimly lighted as to be almost in shadow. An old desk with pigeonholes filled with curled, frayed paper sits in the corner, piled high with a shadowy confusion of books, papers, old keys, scraps of paper, patterns, and the tailor's hat. The tailor sits placidly and patiently in a revolving chair with his back to the desk. The room is made several feet smaller on all sides by stacks of embroidery boards, bolts of fabric, and a clock that reaches from floor to ceiling. A sofa of monstrous beflowered chintz stretches along one side. The girls in their aprons come and go, and the tailor shop waits for the matador past siesta time.

And some day soon, perhaps next Sunday, the beautiful bolero will tell the fate of the matador who comes today. Perhaps the story will begin in the big *corrida* at Madrid

Familiar names on the big corrida

A crimson stain on the pale satin

when the shadows are halfway across the sand and the trumpet calls out with its mournful premonition of tragedy; when the matador steps into the ring in black slippers, white stockings, hair tied with a ribbon, shining in his defenseless armor, to face the black, short-legged, long-horned bull that charges across the white sands of the ring.

Will a crimson stain spread across the pale satin and dull the gold, or will the stiff satin bend in a bow to the crowd as red and pink carnations pile up on the sand?

As the tailor waits, the jewel of the matador's coat glows unperturbed in its box.

The tailor's shop is the beginning of the bullfight for many toreros, the bullfight that too often ends for the matador behind the door of a tiny *capilla* deep in the *corrida*, where the torero comes to his patron saint before he goes into the ring. In the secluded chapel of the *corrida* of Madrid, far behind

Mystery of the Arabian Nights

the glamorous ring, the altar above the slab of marble on the floor blooms with fresh red and pink carnations.

Another door opens onto the *capilla* from a narrow white hallway that connects the *capilla* and the hospital, with its telltale bloodstained pads on the long table in the center of a large room. Too often the matador, in his shining armor, wrapped in his red cape, is carried here from the glory and color of the ring, the band playing *paso dobles,* flowers dotting the sand, and the sound of "Ole, Ole" growing fainter as he passes from the white room through the narrow white hallway to end his young life before the candles in the chapel.

Outside the tailor's shop, the torrid sun whitewashes the buildings; Sevillians move slowly through the narrow streets and disappear behind drawn curtains.

Men are finishing their last glasses of red wine in the *bodega* at the end of the street. The little tables among the wine barrels are emptying. This dimly lighted, cool winery is the *bodega,* or "office," of writers, government men, and politicians. Another café will house doctors and lawyers; another scientists or painters. Here professional men meet and have a *tertulia* (intimate talk), exchange views of their profession, buy and bargain, give legal advice, examine witnesses—and the doctors do everything but operate on the café tables. Everyone knows everyone else's *bodega* as they would his office number, and a man is easier to contact there than a lawyer at 15 Broad Street. There's no secretary to break through. The *chico* takes care of the phone, serves the red wine from the big kegs, and keeps track of the drinks with a piece of chalk on the head of a wine keg, totaling the score at the end of the day under the habitué's initials.

The *bodega* is the Spaniard's office and club, where the price of a few glasses of wine a day pays the rent and the dues. He drinks his wine and has it, too, enjoys the noise and gregarious café life, and carries on business efficiently.

The sun deepens the plaster filigrees of the towers of the Alcazar with shadows, outlines the arches, and touches up the mosaics and gilt. The sun's brightness melds the mixture of the many rebuildings, additions, and restorations of the ancient palace of the Moors, and the mystery and magic of the Arabian Nights fill its halls and passageways. It is to be believed that there *was* a sultan who asked for and received, in return for political aid, one hundred virgins a year, said to have been delivered to its Hall of Maidens. Inside the walls, the duplicate of the old harem is appropriately called Court of Dolls, and the bedchamber of the Moorish kings is resplendent with fourteenth-century gilt and plaster work.

A cool passageway leads from its gardens to Santa Cruz,

A pale water color

the romantic old quarter of Seville. Pristine white houses line narrow streets and enclose small squares filled with orange groves. Balconies overflow with geraniums.

The haze turns Seville into a pale water color, with the almost motionless river forming a lazy loop around the city.

Not far from the Alcazar, the Cathedral of Seville is cool and shadowy inside, with only candles lighting its vastness like fireflies, and its fifty huge pillars disappearing in the darkness of the vaulted ceiling. The choir stall in the center of the cathedral and the tomb of Columbus are separated by great stretches of shadow. After a life of disappointment, Columbus came to final triumph in this resting place, the most spiritual cathedral in the world. If it is possible for mortar and stone to bring one nearer to God, then surely the Cathedral of Seville should bring one the nearest.

At siesta time, it's too hot even to call on the saints, and the cathedral is almost empty.

The elegant Hotel Alfonso XIII across the plaza drowses in the heat.

Soon night will fall, quickly and with a different meaning in Spain than anywhere else. It does not signify the end of day in Seville or Madrid—it's merely the dark part of the afternoon, and three in the morning is the end of the evening.

But the Andalusian farmer sleeps when the sun sleeps, rises when it rises.

The white plaster walls and thatched roof of a small house fight off the blistering Andalusian sun. Inside the door, it's cool and dark where a child plays quietly, with a pottery bowl, on a piece of carpet that covers a square of the dirt floor.

A large bed fills one corner of the room, and along one wall a low chest makes an improvised altar with a fragment of fresh linen and unlighted candles. Four straight chairs sit with their backs against the wall, and on the table in the center of the room is a large basket of brightly colored clothes that are still warm from the sun. The huge cactus that stands in clumps in back of the house is abloom, with other red shirts, blue pants, black cotton dresses, skirts, children's underpants, all sticking to the big thorny leaves, drying in the sun.

While the sleepy, black-eyed child rolls languidly on the cool floor, his mother draws water in a bucket from a well in back of the house, and in the shade of the lean-to kitchen she washes the big green cucumbers to prepare the *gazpacho* (oil soup) for the evening meal. She watches the patchwork of little fields past the cactus fence for the signal to make José and the other men their bread-and-beans lunch and opens a jug of welcome red wine. A black mongrel growls and slinks from shade to shade as the sun moves in the heat-hazy sky.

Across a scrap of reddish-black earth three plows move abreast, one pulled by a bedraggled donkey, one by an ancient horse, and one by an ox. Other farmers had come to help José dig a living from his reluctant land, as he would in turn help them with his treasured ox.

At the ends of brown, moist furrows lie the water jugs keeping cool in the damp, newly turned earth.

Beyond the rolling hills behind the fields, the valley gives up its straggly vegetation entirely to the chalk hills around Jerez de la Frontera, where the land so willingly gives life to roses as big as cabbages, clouds of wisteria, and the grapes that are turned into Spain's heady sherry in the winery of Gonzalez Byass & Co. There humor is mixed with wine making. The kegs in one cellar are named for kings and queens, ambassadors, and movie stars, and twelve barrels in

Humor and wine making

. . . inside, cool and dark

a row are inscribed for the apostles. For Winston Churchill, a barrel of his favorite sherry is inscribed: "To Methuselah on Sir Winston's 80th Birthday." Queen Elizabeth and former ambassador John Davis Lodge have namesakes, too.

But on the other side of the little valley across which the thatch-roofed cottages straggle lies Seville. Once José had been to the beautiful city. He remembers it well and hopes he may go again before he is too old—a year when his fields are good—and take his wife and children to show them the sights he has seen. They'd go to the great cathedral, walk past the fine houses and peek in at the gardens and the colored-tile patios through the iron gates, even go into the Alcazar. And up and down the narrow Calle Sierpes with the unbelievable things that sparkle and shine in the windows—the mantillas and velvets.

They would walk slowly past the *bodega* where men were laughing, talking, and drinking red wine which perfumed the street; past the little windows where girls were embroidering patterns on satins with thread that shone like silver and gold. They'd cross the big square and stand inside the lacy iron gate on the pebble drive of the Hotel Alfonso XIII, where men in gold braid and white gloves guard the door, and watch the shiny cars come and go. They'd take their lunch in the shade of the tangerine trees in María Luisa Park and see its big half-moon lake of water, there just to reflect the big white Plaza de España.

But these are the things José talks about to his wife in the warm Andalusian night when they sit in the lean-to kitchen, tired and content, their children asleep in the big bed.

Each section of Spain is like a different country, each of its historical cities as different as the painter each city claims. Murillo is said to be the painter of Seville; El Greco of Toledo; and Goya of Madrid.

Seville is warm and soft in color, and friendly. Toledo is a city of stone, blending with the stone of the hills; its jagged towers, spires, and gray ruins are barren and bleached. Almost surrounded by the Tagus River, it's now a fortress of treasures, the whole city declared a national monument.

A fortress of treasu

The Cathedral of Toledo, overpoweringly ornate, is swarming with priests, tourists, children, and vendors. With all its reredos, carved pulpits, and magnificent grillwork, statuary, and gold, it has lost that spiritual quality so moving in the Cathedral of Seville.

The White Virgin—probably the most beautiful of all the statues of the Virgin; the choir stalls, with each seat differently carved; the Virgin of the Sagrario; El Greco's The Spoliation; the carved figure of St. Francis of Assisi; and the gold monstrance, made of the first gold from America, are only a few of the treasures of the Cathedral of Toledo.

The narrow streets are picturesque, running up and down and spiraling around the mountainous hills, past little cafés and quaint houses that are very elegantly furnished inside by rich landowners who summer in Toledo. Toledo, though a cultural center, has the cold, unlived-in quality of the monument that it is.

El Greco's home and garden are still intact, furnished with

Nuns and El Greco's
Tears of St. Peter

some of the original furnishings and authentic pieces of his time. On the easel in the painter's studio is one of his five great paintings of the Tears of St. Peter. The kitchen is complete with pottery and pans, and in the large hall are El Greco's famous paintings of the twelve apostles. Next to this is the El Greco Museum, small but filled with treasures. One small room is dominated with a huge sculpture of Christ on the cross, strange and pagan in black robe edged in gilt. Behind these two ancient doors of El Greco's house and museum, on a street so narrow and steep as to be accessible only on foot, are many of the immortal paintings the great painter gave to Spain, the land of his adoption.

Along the ocher clay roads and rock hills toward Madrid is the palace of the Duchess of Lerma. Back of the beautiful, old, iron-studded doors is a private museum which can be seen only by special permission, by request through the family or government. Here is El Greco's unfinished Baptism of Christ, which he was painting at the time of his death.

Here also is the famous painting of The Bearded Lady, which was commissioned as proof of this phenomenon; the great painter made the unattractive commission into a touching masterpiece. In the Duchess's private apartments are other rare paintings and art treasures. The Duchess's bedroom is in dark-green velvet and satin, with a huge, intricately patterned silver jewel case. The walls are covered with priceless paintings. In the drawing room, for some unknown reason, in the midst of all the elegant furnishings is an overstuffed Grand Rapids sofa and two chairs.

Toward Madrid the red-clay hills are covered with gray olive trees, and only an occasional village huddles along the dusty road, its gardens and cobblestone courtyards hidden behind walls. Scattered houses face the road with their elegant old carved wooden doors, and finally the land smooths out and lies flat and green. Madrid—the city of Goya—suddenly appears on the stark plains against the cloudless sky.

. . . in the steep, narrow streets

Madrid—realistic, imaginative, and colorful, with a definiteness of manners and people and physical appearance portrayed in sharp, well-defined lines. Though it has some of the delightful fluid charm of Seville, it has also some of the rigid qualities of Toledo.

The city does not drift, but appears suddenly out of the landscape. It has no straggling suburbs nor appendages, but it has that architectural blight that is plaguing all cities of the world: cement-block "tenement modern," standing in rows and bunches of dozens, as if each building were trying to hide behind the other. In various stages of completion they stand, sometimes painted like billboards vying for attention, always surrounded by huge clay holes ready to receive other gray shafts. In Madrid they rise out of the placid landscape and surround the gentle city as they do in Paris, less in Athens, more in Rome, Beirut, and Hong Kong.

The beautiful city of Madrid lies unperturbed: lacy-grilled, balconied, white houses wearing roof gardens like flowered hats; potted geraniums in tiled patios, each with its own private cat; and tree-lined streets, misty fountains, and parks guarded by graceful statues.

Dignified buildings are watched over by the stately Prado Museum, creating a city so harmonious as to have been built by one architect, but with the endless imagination of a thousand artists. Spain is a country of individuals, independence, and strong personalities. They have shaped the Spanish way of life: the extreme privacy of their home life; the lateness of their night life; the aloofness of their social life, evidenced in their refusal to coop themselves up in offices all day when they can do business in their cafés and *bodegas* on the broad avenues and plazas while they sip *sangrias,* and in their urban way of living—not constantly chasing the taillight of another car to rush to the country for weekends; no suburbia, with commuting to take time away from leisure.

The Spanish are seemingly austere and aloof, but are above all delightfully gay, and thrive on fun and noise. Their strong personalities come through and give color to every side of Spanish life, as Baltasar Iban's personal hospitality and enthusiasm for Americans can be felt the moment you step foot in the door of his Wellington Hotel. Many floors below the ground his tiled kitchens are filled with the latest American gadgets—grills, freezers, beaters, whippers and coolers. "The Farm" outside Madrid (where the Baltasars spend much of their time) sets the gourmet tables of the dining room and El Fogon restaurant of the hotel.

Acres of flatlands surround "The Farm," which is a marvel of pedigreed ducks in scientific igloos, chickens in glass houses and beef born and bred in tiled stalls with running water. The California ranch house where we started luncheon on seafood delicacies and rare white wine is complete with swimming pool, tall slim trees and flowers, with its own little chapel nearby. The garage houses prized American cars.

Huge fluffy sheep dogs, the size of fighting bulls (which are raised on other Iban ranches) stand guard at the gates and roam the grounds. And unless you want a sheep dog for your living room don't admire them too much, as someone I know in St. Louis did and one of the huge beasts arrived by plane a month later—a gift from Baltasar and his lovely blond wife. Baltasar, like most Spaniards, is generous, madly interested in the game of business; an indefatigable perfectionist with a gay façade that makes work seem like play.

Along the ocher hills
. . . a house faces the road

France

A BATTLE RAGES IN THE GARDEN

Behind this château door a battle rages in the garden. Beyond the stone steps that quickly descend to the grass terrace, past the militant rows of trees where the mirrored canal duplicates the pale sky and the budding willows—there, at the bottom of the garden, a battle rages.

Among the lichen-dappled statues, the hoofs of rearing horses churn the fresh green grass, trample the flowers; the shields of the unhorsed clash; plumes wave, armor flickers, and swords flash.

The U-shaped château faces away from the garden on a huge stone courtyard. Along one side are the sumptuous stables, and the other wing is the kitchen and the servants' quarters.

But what of the battle in the garden?

It will still be raging as long as there is a Frenchman like André (my delightful escort) to tell the stormy, often macabre, history of France that's been fought out on every rolling hillside, in each valley, at every drawbridge. And there'll always be an André, with his leather gloves flapping at the wrist, his Homburg on the side of his head, and the eternal cigarette to point out the fleeing enemy as he disappears through the *allée* in the forest where every Frenchman's ancestors fought to defend their lands and their châteaux.

On every riverbank an invader camps; through every forest rides a conqueror. From every corner of France her lustrous history leaps from the mouths of the crumbling aristocracy, the peasant, the newly rich, the young. Every château, palace, and castle tells of a lover imprisoned, a mistress's revenge, a queen beheaded, a king dethroned.

True, this all happened centuries ago, but the battles of France, the intrigue, the splendor, like the French kings, never die.

As a background for this romantic history, so familiar to the world in every detail, the ancient and inimitable French talent for landscaping has preserved the unsurpassed beauty of France, unchanged for centuries, by rearranging Nature, a co-operation with, rather than a contradiction of, the

Plumes wave . . . armor flickers

natural landscape: gardens painted with water stretched into ribbon-like canals and coaxed into lakes, pools, and waterfalls; a group of poplars arranged in a semicircle; shrubs and flowers gathered into bouquets; forests rearranged in rows (every tree in France must surely have felt the shears and the clippers); and poplar trees draped like a gauzy curtain in front of a timid village. On the countryside of France is engraved a vivid and beautiful memory of the past blended with the present. Even the working landscape—the canals on which the slim barges drift across the meadows, filled with cargoes of wood, coal, potatoes; great work horses clomping home from the fields at dusk in the rain; a peasant still plowing in the fields—has a quality of belonging to the past.

It would not seem at all strange to behold Charlemagne and his army galloping over a hillock along the Marne. And the horses of the king's carriage racing along the Bouquet de la Roi to Fontainebleau, with the black leather and brass of the harness gleaming, the curtains drawn, would be less incongruous than the stark skyscraper that scars the entrance to Fontainebleau. André agrees.

The narrow cobblestone roads still wind through the forests around Chantilly. It would be no surprise to hear the clattering of the carriage of the Duc de Marigny racing eagerly in the falling rain to gay Chantilly. To be sure, André, like any Frenchman, would toot his horn (allowed in the country) or shout the footman to one side to make sure he didn't have to reduce his own wildly speeding Citroën.

At Chantilly the steaming horses would go from the château to the Grandes Ecuries, the most luxurious stables ever built and one of the most beautiful examples of eighteenth-century architecture in France. The domed rotunda, the huge marble fountain for the horses to drink from, bronze deer decorating the walls, statues in the courtyard, antlers ornamenting the stalls—all so elegant that the Duc d'Aumale is said to have remarked when the stalls were built that the Duke of Bourbon, for whom the stables were designed, must have expected to be reincarnated as a horse. Now the stables look snobbishly down on the bangtails that earn their hay at the Chantilly race track.

The castles of France, the gardens, the treasures, the cathedrals, the monasteries, the dungeons, torture chambers, and sculpture of the past still stand. The vistas are still cut clean and straight through the forests. The placid canals are waiting, the fountains at Versailles leap and play, the paths of Fontainebleau are raked; the hedges are clipped and the smell of fresh-cut grass fills the air—and the elegant, the frivolous men and women of France's past are still there.

Many of the old wines of France lie asleep in ancient caves

The paths of Fontainebleau are raked

where the fertile black soil of the Marne Valley gives way to the chalk plains around Epernay, where the story of sparkling champagne begins. Though at times the vines have been destroyed by foreign raiders or by the dreaded vine blight, always the grapes of this region and the wine masters bring forth the same inimitable sparkling champagne. This gift of the grapes turns time back to the seventeenth century, when the monk, Dom Pérignon, in the Benedictine monastery of Hautvillers produced a slightly sparkling *cuvée,* or vatting. The champagne that now fills the fifteen miles of black, quiet caves of Moët-Chandon can be said to be the direct descendant of that sparkling wine.

André, who never wearies of food in any form, introduced me to artichoke heart topped with egg and caviar, but agreed that no mention of French food should ever be made unless you intend to devote several volumes to it.

France's history has no villains and no heroes; kings never die, and their glamorous mistresses and their lovers, painters, poets, warriors, and chefs live on forever and, the French generation after generation, move among their shadows. Nowhere in the ancient or modern world does this atmosphere exist as it does in France. The Buddhist gods are always present and the patron saints of the Catholics hover over all, but France's decadent and deathless past lives in every house, walks every street, duels in every garden.

André doesn't agree.

True, give a Frenchman a juicy tidbit of politics to chew, a fast car to drive, or delicious food and wine, and he lives in the present. Two Frenchwomen left with a bit of romantic gossip are lost in the future. And at the sunny seaside the French leave their ancestors behind and plunge into the water with their bare-topped children and their bikinis.

André, who smokes five packages of cigarettes a day, has never learned the length nor the strength of the ash. The seat of our car looked more like a burning ghat than the new, fish-faced Citroën that slithered along the road at breakneck speed. Smoke billowed from the windows as if we were cooking lunch inside. Small villages whizzed by, which André pointed out with his cigarette: Barbizon, where the poets came; Senlis, with the beautiful cathedral hidden away in

Direct descendant of Dom Pérignon's cuvée

No mention of food

In the palace, 10-watt bulbs

the little town among the lace-curtained cottages and elegant houses behind walls (once the whole town was walled, an important bastion of Paris)—the little houses across the countryside hiding their faces, defying the intrusion of prying eyes into the poorest French peasant's beloved privacy.

Independence, the motivating desire of a Frenchman's life, makes him demand privacy almost as much as comfort. Yet many of the stately châteaux can be seen through—into the vast windows on one side and right out the other side—and are designed so that it is necessary to go through one room to get to another, sometimes in a long string of rooms opening only onto one another. Surrounding these transparent châteaux are deep moats, high walls, and battalions of trees.

If the French countryside—from the Mediterranean to the wine valleys, through the wheat lands, the pasture lands and ranches, the villages and farms—is under the spell of the past romance of France, Paris is even more so. In Paris, grandeur is a state of mind and formality a necessity. Every other door or house is a national monument, including the walls inside Maxim's and the Petit Palais Bourbon. And Brigitte Bardot may be declared a national monument any day.

The first door on the left wing of the Petit Palais Bourbon is one of the most beloved doors of Paris to many people all over the world, particularly Americans, for it leads to hospitality rarely known in Paris. The French, like the Japanese—but for different reasons—do not share their homes freely.

Once through these doors in the cobblestone passageway, you find that the first door to the right opens on a winding stairway with plaster-patched walls, dimly lighted with the usual ten-watt bulbs (made especially for French landlords). "French landlords never repair," André explained, "for any improvement would attract the unfavorable and costly attention of the tax collector."

The doors on the second and third floors have indications as to where the light button is and various little plaques of information, but no clue as to the number of the apartment or the name of the occupant. The Palais Bourbon has too long been occupied by the same people for anything so mundane. The butler on the second floor is very helpful.

When the third-floor door opens, Marie Louise Bousquet's warmth and vivaciousness light the stairway like a thousand-watt bulb. She speaks in English that is so French and French that is so explicit it's scarcely discernible when she switches, as she constantly does, from one language to the other in the middle of a sentence.

The old parquet floors glow softly, and warm light fills the entresol. But the drawing room is very decisive, with a black-and-white tapestry rug; sharp green glass vases, like crème de menthe, monopolize a white marble mantel; and scarlet brocade satin at the windows shuts out the lights of the Place de Bourbon. A grand piano, staggering under flowers and photographs of the famous, the fashionable, the titled, the talented, and the just plain rich, takes up a good part of the room. But another small parlor opens onto this to catch the overflow of guests. Here Marie Louise, in a blue Chanel suit with white silk shirt, the cuffs linked in fabulous gold, sits on a low chair and talks animatedly. Her hair and eyes are exactly the color of real henna, her eyes filled with fire. On the walls are paintings by Braque and young French artists; a magnificent portrait of Marie Louise by Blanc; and a huge Bernard Buffet rooster done in his flaying black-and-white style.

In this little apartment Marie Louise Bousquet, Paris editor of *Harper's Bazaar,* hostess extraordinaire, has been introducing the world to the world at her Thursday salons for many years.

"Marie Louise's guest book would bring real money in Paris or New York," André commented.

Gabrielle Chanel's salon door is a fashion landmark. But the door that makes fashion is the little door reflected in the multi-mirrored staircase that turns the three floors of her salon into a dazzling "Alice through the Looking-Glass."

When the crowds are vying for chairs or a place to stand at an opening and the fashion greats have arrived—Carmel Snow, Jessica Daves, Nancy White, Willa Cushman, Sally Kirkland, Becky Hamilton, Bettina Ballard, Henry Sell, Mel Dawley, Andrew Goodman, Hector Escobosa, Vee Rafdal, Marlene Dietrich—then Chanel takes her place on the top step of the stair, like a child listening to forbidden conversation below.

Reflected a hundred times in the mirrors is a small door at the top of the stairs . . . a door through which no one enters. Here Mme. Chanel creates fashions for the world. . . . Seated on the top step before the door, she watches the mannequins descend the stairs. In the mirror she sees the faces of the crowd seated in the room below in the

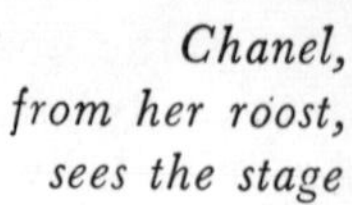

Chanel,
from her roost,
sees the stage

Bardot a national monument?

velvet and gilt chairs. By the time a mannequin reaches the antique screen of the stage, Chanel, from her roost, knows if that gown is a success.

Along the Rue Royale, the bronze doors designed by Jacques Gabriel, who created the Opéra of Louis XV at Versailles for the king, have long been declared national monuments and cannot be disturbed by their owners. Number 8 was originally the private house of the great architect, and is today the home of Christofle's famous silver, now at home too on New York's 57th Street.

An emerald bracelet can be kept a secret

On the Rue de la Paix, not a national monument but of a special vintage, is Cartier's, modern black marble and gilt façade. Inside all is quiet; the gray rugs and gray velvet drapes look like the inside of those little velvet and satin boxes jewels come in. In these small rooms, splattered with crystal chandeliers and secluded alcoves, are the world's most beautiful jewels—not the crown jewels, the national treasury, or the emerald Buddha, but jewels that are worn by the most elegant women in the world. There is one small room, all hush-hush and eloquently quiet, where a diamond ring could be selected in privacy, an emerald bracelet kept a secret until it dangled mysteriously from the wrong wrist.

A million francs is all you need to dine in any one of the hundreds of wonderful Paris restaurants, but the trick is to find a place that's really French, really good, and a secret. Ferris Megarity took me to Brasserie Lipp, into which half of Paris is crushed after the theater. (It's no secret but great fun.) The search among André's friends finally led me to 14 Boulevard St. Germain, a country restaurant with sausages, each in a white paper diaper, hanging from the ceiling over the heads of the guests. Two steps inside the door is a short bar where René presides. Your coat is whisked away and you are standing with a Beaujolais apéritif in your hand. Once you are at the table, René, in his sweater, is everywhere at once, taking an umbrella, adding a chair, pouring

Petit point in the elevator

wine, giving orders—a happy Frenchman. Pale country butter the size of a slice of pie shows up with fresh bread. Tiny frogs' legs the size of shrimp, as tender as custard; poulet with wine sauce and braised endive; chocolate mousse; or a dozen other things. A vendor moves in, under the eye of René, for one trip around, selling red roses and violets. Waiters in black waistcoats and shirt sleeves, with black aprons, speak only French—and so does René.

The smartest woman I saw in Paris was here—a silver blonde, not young, not old, hair cut and draped like a piece of chiffon, informally dressed in a pale blue tweed dress, with one smart pin of clear white diamonds. Diamonds and sausage? But René's good food and intimate atmosphere give diamonds and sausage a common cause.

The next evening a friend from England asked me to dine. As I descended in the petit-point lined antique elevator of the Hotel Meurice to meet him, I debated whether I should tell him about René's and decided against doing so. In the cab he told me we were dining at a little restaurant that few foreigners knew about. He confided the address to the cabbie: 14 Boulevard St. Germain. I discovered eight Americans who are keeping it a secret. Thibaut de Saint Phalle, who knows more about Paris than anyone should, said, "Of course I know it. I lunched there when I was in Paris last week."

Diamonds and sausages, a common cause

Italy

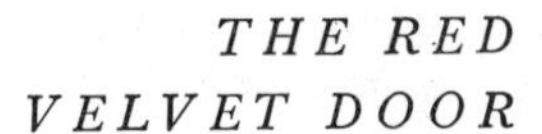

THE RED VELVET DOOR

THE DOOR above the entrance to St. Peter's was hung with crimson velvet, as it is on the most special occasions of solemn benedictions when the Pope appears on the balcony before the crowds in the Piazza San Pietro.

It was Easter morning and the piazza was a mosaic of rain-polished umbrellas of every color. Priests and nuns huddled under big umbrellas in black groups, scarcely discernible one from the other. Rome was blurred by the veil of rain. The water slid over the stone pavement and gushed through the crevices between the stones, driven by the beating rain down the gently sloping piazza to the colonnades. Women no longer stepped gingerly from stone to stone on tiptoes, but settled down in their soaked slippers that squished with water.

Rain ran down the back of one person from the umbrella of another. For two hours the crowd had grown, and now stood motionless, facing the red velvet door. Waiting. Barricaded at the steps, the cathedral was filled to overflowing. The colonnades sprouted more umbrellas. The crowd no longer resisted the rain but became a part of it, unmindful as it dripped down their sleeves and eddied around their feet. They became a continuation of the rain on its undeterred way to the earth. The contours of the huge figures above the façade of the basilica that overlooks the piazza were softened by the blur of rain, and the pillars of the loggia glistened.

The rain, like a catalyst, united the shining umbrellas, the dripping people, the basilica, the pillars, the stones, concentrating them all into one motionless mass, with the only movement that of the rain. Only the voluptuous curtains, like a fresh red mouth in a weeping, gray, lined face, seemed to be outside the reach of the rain. At twelve noon the curtain stirred, like a mouth about to form a word. A figure passed like a shadow in front of the curtain. The Latin words came over the loud-speaker above the pounding rain, but diffused as if they too had mingled with the rain, and finally the words of benediction fell, separated into tiny spaces between the silver drops that splashed onto the umbrellas, sprayed onto the crowds, touched their faces.

The voice stopped. The mosaic of umbrellas cracked, broke up, as the crowd turned its face away from the red velvet door. Their eyes were shining as if the rain had reached into them. People poured from the shelter of the cathedral, but their eyes were shining too.

From a hill above the city of Rome miles away, other eyes are looking at St. Peter's through the famous keyhole of the doors of the Villa dei Cavalieri di Malta.

These doors to the walled garden of the Villa of the Knights of Malta have been closed for a hundred years, and the key no doubt long ago lost. But through the keyhole, Michelangelo's exquisite dome of St. Peter's is seen like a jewel, set apart by the circle of the keyhole that frames the garden path of the villa, overhung by bordering trees, providing a vista that encloses the dome.

The path, lined with close-set trees, forms a telescope that gives to the scene a strangely detailed dimension—the look of a perfect white cameo set among intricately carved green leaves.

Down the years, as the keyhole has framed the cameo of St. Peter's for the eye, the metal lock has worn shiny from the cheeks that have brushed against it.

Through the keyhole —Michelangelo

Since the fifth century the musical doors to the Chapel of St. John the Baptist have bewitched the ear. In the Piazza Laterano is the church of San Giovanni in the Fountain, the oldest baptistry in Rome.

Enclosing the church are magnificent porphyry columns. Here, at the entrance to the Chapel of St. John the Baptist, are the heavy bronze doors that show signs of hidden gold and silver inlays and are so constructed that, when slowly opened, they play the notes of the scale. This might be construed by the less erudite as a squeaking door, but the doors do indeed repeat the same distinct scale-like notes each time.

Dining in a national monument, lifting a *campari* cocktail among the art treasures of a museum, or dancing in a restored basilica are not unusual around the world, especially in Rome. Through the modern door of the Ulpia Restaurant and Taverna, two flights of worn stone steps lead down to the restored remnants of the Basilica Ulpia, vintage 111 A.D. The stone floors, parts of walls, steps, and some of the statuary are all now part of the restaurant.

Inside the dining salon, boned chicken is turned golden in herbs and flaming brandy at the table and served with tiny sweet peas and blood oranges and Nicilla wine. Just outside the door, the Parian marble Trajan column stands proudly in the ruins of the once six-story Trajan market where Marcus Aurelius held auctions, selling the treasures of the imperial treasury to finance the Marcomannic War. The statue of Trajan the Emperor once stood on the column's lofty peak, a place now occupied by St. Peter, and at its feet it once sheltered the golden coffin of Hadrian. From its tower, the bell tolled for the Greek monks in the little church of S. Nicolò della Colonna, which stood at its base.

Evening begins and ends early in Rome. At eleven o'clock, when the Spanish and the Egyptians are just beginning dinner, it is cabaret time in Rome.

A rain-polished cab drives as close as possible to the blue marquee of the Hostería dell'Orso. Dozens of other cabs have wound through the tiny cobblestone streets on this rainy spring evening to deposit the fashionables of Rome at what is probably the world's most lush night spot, virtually hidden

. opening with the scale

Below, the Basilica Ulpia

away below street level, along the Tiber River at Ponte Umberto.

In the Middle Ages travelers from all parts of the world stopped at the Hostería dell'Orso, Rome's famous Inn of the Bear. Among its guests was St. Francis of Assisi; Dante lived there during the Jubilee Year; and in 1400 Rabelais, Goethe, and Montaigne were its guests.

As centuries passed, the Hostería fell into ill repute with a history of lurid murders and stories of bodies entombed in the walls.

In 1940 Toni Prantera reopened the inn as a night club, and fashionable Rome happily returned to its secluded charm. Still intact through the centuries are the thirteenth-century beams, stairways, and floors that set off the satin and velvet décor and glow in the candlelight. Cars and cabs cautiously maneuver in its tiny cobblestone courtyard. The Hostería has been declared a national monument, and no change can be made in the 550-year-old inn.

Behind the blue marquee, candle chandeliers light a blue, velvet, and gold cocktail lounge. Scarlet-carpeted stairs lead to a dining salon, and the third floor is the fabulous Cabala cabaret. Deep rugs and velvet-hung doorways muffle that indescribable, inimitable music that comes only out of Italy. Chic Italian men, the best-dressed in the world, and women with the newest haircuts and the most elegant clothes, worn with that great ease that makes Italian women truly among the most chic of all women, pass under the blue marquee.

At the back-door terrace in an old palazzo on the Via Gregoriana, three young girls in their white smocks with black pincushion belts sit in the sun and gossip at lunch time. Others walk in twos and threes up and down the slanting street past the palazzo that is the maison of Simonetta. Inside the honey-beige, chandeliered salon, chic young girls are showing fabulous clothes to big American store buyers.

Chic Italian women are in fitting rooms approving custom-made fashions. Simonetta arrives in the beige salon besieged by her staff for approval of a detail, about a customer to see, a phone to answer, a new fabric—Simonetta, handsome and vibrant, manages all things at once.

Born the Duchess Colonna di Cesaro, Simonetta, twice married, with two sons, a great house on the Appia Antica, and a life filled with social activity, is at her atelier every morning designing clothes, her love since childhood.

At twenty-four, Simonetta was the youngest Italian couturière, with her own maison. Vogue, Bergdorf Goodman, and Marshall Field were first to discover her for America and

Thirteenth-century beams, and sweet music

The back door of an old palazzo

since then the Palazzo on Via Gregoriana has influenced fashion in every country where there is fashion.

Donna Simonetta, always an independent thinker (as was her father), defied the Fascist regime and was twice imprisoned during its time.

Not far from Simonetta's maison starts the S-curved Via Venéto, the street of cafés. About five blocks long, it's probably one of the shortest and undoubtedly the smartest street in Rome. Nowhere are there more attractive people. The cafés, where people talk from table to table and meet in groups for a before-lunch or a five o'clock apéritif, run the full length of some blocks, one touching another. The narrow space of sidewalk between tables is almost impassable.

Here everyone in Rome meets everyone else. The fashionable Flora Hotel overlooks the street from the top. A crowd blocks the street to glimpse a princess alighting from a car in the arch of the Excelsior. Bruce Cabot is sitting at exactly the same table where I saw him three years ago, and seems to be known by everyone at every table. The Via Venéto is the gaily beating heart of Rome.

Here we joined Renata Signorini to cross the street to his atelier up above the Via Venéto among the red tile roofs and treetops, a Roman penthouse-studio of a modern-day Roman sculptor, where all that glitters *is* gold. For behind this door on the roof is the big, dark-paneled studio where Signorini sculpts in miniature in 24-carat gold punctuated

A fountain in every square

All that glitters is *gold*

with precious stones. A bust of Clare Boothe Luce wearing a jeweled brooch looks with green emerald eyes from a glass case. A golden Audrey Hepburn with a ruby tiara in her hair, diamond-adorned Princess Soraya; Princess Grace of Monaco, Peggy Hitchcock, and Sophia Loren are created in one-third life size; all busts have sapphire or emerald eyes and are restrainedly bejeweled.

America's Tiffany presented Signorini's golden image of Her Majesty to Queen Elizabeth—one hundred and twenty-five thousand dollars in bullion and jewels. On the clay easel in the big studio room are the beginnings of figures in gold forming the Nativity, which will some day come to Tiffany's.

Flowers bloom in Rome

A stage the size of two Cadillacs

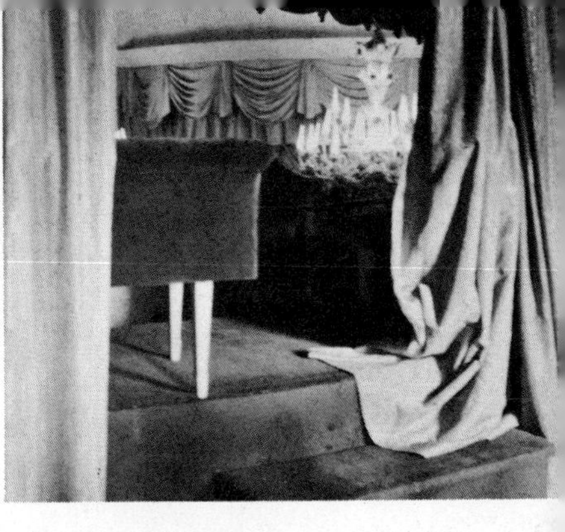

Besides portrait sculpture in gold, Signorini has done exquisite figures of the Madonna, saints, and decorative miniature statues. After many years of life-size sculpturing, Signorini turned to the idea of the golden and bejeweled miniatures as a decorative and personalized form of art, and also for his very good reason: "Today, who has room for life-size sculpture and marble horses in small apartments and town houses?" Gone are the marble halls and galleries for statuary, gone the fountains and gateways, the colonnades—those are only for commercial decoration.

When Signorini's collection was shown at Tiffany's America was stirred by it, and now Signorini is immortalizing in gold and emeralds those who can afford to spend their gold and have it too.

The loge curtains are drawn aside in the tiny Teátro della Cométa, and the soft reflections of the chandeliers turn the theater into a perfect pearl suspended in the center of an old mansion near the Campidoglio.

The Teátro della Cométa is exquisite in detail, in its modern way, as much a little gem as Marie Antoinette's little theater at the Petite Trianon. The pearl moiré silk lining from dome to floor, rose-velvet lounges, and velvety carpets.

The stage is the size of two Cadillacs side by side, but by scenic and staging ingenuity the stage accommodates a stage within a stage for *Le Tram Delúse*.

From the lobby, where hors d'oeuvres and drinks are served, the garden can be seen—flagstone paths among flowers, hedges and a bubbling fountain. Teátro della Cométa, which seats only a hundred and fifty, is a gathering place of Roman and international society.

A gauzy curtain of water falls in front of a secluded grotto in the gardens of the Villa d'Este in Tívoli. The villa with its frescoed loggia faces the garden; the Bernini fountain; the Avenue of Fountains, each of the one hundred different fountains emptying into the fabulous flow of waterfalls, fountains, and pools that interlace the gardens; a bannister of waterfalls that follows the stone stair from the villa to the bottom of the garden; the tallest cypress trees in Italy; flowers and hedges; the Rotunda dei Cypressi.

From the Zuccari-frescoed loggias, the villa looks over the valley that surrounds beautiful Tívoli; Rocca Pia, the fifteenth-century fortress; the hillsides with a net of grapevines laid over them. Underneath the villa are great tunnels in the solid rock, carrying the water that the artistry of Bernini and others trained into falls and taught to jump into the air and fall in patterns, to lie quietly in shallow pools and reflect the sky.

All this power was engineered by direction and restraint of the natural course of the rushing water in the gorges descending from the mountaintop.

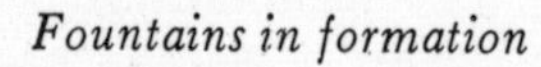

Fountains in formation

A doorway of water

An old woman disappears

Surrounding the once-elegant summer villa on the mountain with its cooling fountains are the winding streets and passages of the old town of Tívoli. At the topmost peak on the mountain, one of these little streets ends in a small cobblestone piazza where the sun comes to light half the little square with a white heat, while the other half of the square is stubbornly protected by the little houses that hold it in their cool shadows.

In a doorway that rises on stone steps above the rough courtyard, a woman sits on a low chair, sewing, and another leans against the steps. The wash is hung on the line and lunch is over. Children play in their only yard, the courtyard. A man in a wheel chair, a veteran of the last war, looks quietly into the blue, cloudless sky.

The old woman is shy and, gathering her sewing in her apron, disappears inside. The curtain billows out from the doorway and the man in the wheel chair turns and smiles. A group of little girls in big white hair bows and blue convent uniforms huddle together and giggle.

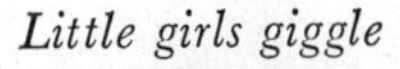
Little girls giggle

Greece

THE FALLEN DOORS OF GREECE AND THE GUIDE SNOBS

THERE'S a new class of snobs to add to the wine snobs, the clothes snobs, the handmade-shoe snobs, the art snobs, and the hotel snobs who can make a whole evening sound like Robert Warner's directory of distinguished hotels in Europe. This new species, the Guide Snob, returns from distant lands with stories not of what they saw, but of their guides—the penniless countess in Rome; the pretty Thai girl; the college girl in Turkey; the old major in Agra—who made their trips a success and were the only natives the travelers got to know. Good guides are becoming as well known among travelers as the right dressmakers in Hong Kong, the pearl shops in Japan, and that little hotel in Jakarta.

A guide—which I usually avoid—is a must with many travelers, becoming oracle, companion, confidant, and mark of distinction; photographic assistant, holding the telescopic lens while the traveler shoots with the wide focus; and leading him to a cheese sandwich when he cannot nibble another raw fish or balance another grain of rice on a chopstick.

This expensive "pig in a poke" travel adjunct with whom you can spend your days makes it worth while to get a few names and addresses from the guide snobs. What you too often get, from what I have heard and know from my limited experience, is a disinterested character who speaks neither his nor your native language. The only English he speaks is "Yes" when you ask him if he speaks English. He doesn't know where the pyramids are (because he's bored with going there); he knows where the Temple of the Emerald Buddha is but takes you to Wat Po because it is nearer. He knows where the Thieves' Market is but doesn't know how to get there. Never heard of your hotel once you're out of sight of it. Knows all the long ways round to every place, particularly past the library, the post office, new gymnasium, and his girl friend's house (to see if any guys are hanging around), the waterworks, and other fascinating places you're dying not to see. He'll always take the road along the railroad freight yards instead of along the sea, but he can count like a whiz by 2–4–6–8s when the day's bill is totaled up to more than it cost to come from the U.S. You spend all your time watching the map, finding the places, and he sees the scenery.

I found guide snobs are made, not born. My travels have always been "guided" by friends, new-found and old, as they were in Greece. But Spiro, my self-appointed Greek guide, was the connecting link from place to place, person to person, who turned out to be my timetable, accountant, driver; who held my handbag while I used my camera, held both while I used my compact; fished the right coins out of handfuls of lires, escudos, francs, guilders, shillings, pesetas, telephone slugs, and pennies; paid fees and haggled over prices.

My first day in Athens, I sat at a table in the Grande Bretagne café with Jeanne Baseos, who had brought a huge bouquet of blue, red, purple, and pink anemones from her garden for me. Her uncle, A. A. Pallis, joined us. They set my life in motion in Athens and it never stopped. Philip and Shirlee Messinesi in New York turned the key.

But it was Spiro who waited for hours at the Acropolis, where, from the Parthenon, so close to the blue sky, I saw Athens for the first time: a white city stretching over the hills in the sun in elegant palm-dotted avenues to the blue sea, interchangeable with the sky between the hills. Saw Athens to remember, through the ancient doorway of the Propylaea, which has remained unfinished since 431 B.C., without sculpture or carved facade because the priests of Brauronion would not permit one wing of the building to spread into the sacred area of their temples. Stark and majestic the doorway stands, passing from incompletion to ruins.

Among the ancient stones of the Citadel, a poppy grows by the Parthenon, bravely measuring its beauty beside a huge stone rosette which has blossomed for centuries in the green grass. Yellow field flowers grow in the crevices, halfway up the stone wall of the Acropolis and along the fragments of marble steps to hide the scars of time.

Along the grassy slopes of the hill of the Acropolis on the way to the ruins of the Dionysos Theater, lie elegantly fringe-carved columns, overgrown with tall grass. A scarlet geranium blossoms against the drapery of the stone like a flower stuck in the folds of a bodice.

A brave young tree

A poppy grows by the Parthenon

Farther along the path the steep hillside turns to stone and marble, describing the remains of an amphitheater. Up a short flight of steps cut from the stone over two thousand years ago, I stepped through what was once the doorway to the ancient stage of the Dionysos Theater, considered the most important monument of the fourth century in Greece as the only remaining ruins of a theater with a circular orchestra, with the exception of Epidaurus, where the summer festivals are held.

The relief of figures supporting the stage still stand. Socrates lay beside the steps, in a heap of his own making.

Here under the stars, overlooking the flowering hills and the olive groves, on the marble stage curtained by cypress in the shadow of the Parthenon, tragedies of the greatest ancient authors were performed more than two thousand years ago.

More than 2000 years ago

Some of the stone chairs of the theater are intact, carved in different designs, with shaped seats and massive arms.

A few moments' drive from Acropolis hill, a forgotten backstage light spotlighted a doorway slightly ajar. The play was over and the National Theater in Athens was in darkness. The rows of red velvet seats in the tiny circular theater were littered with programs that made a small white blur in the dim light from an exit door. The few rows of the balcony were in blackness.

The backstage doorway stood as it was pulled off the stage at the end of the second act of the Spanish drama. The brokenhearted señorita, a crumpled note in her hand, wept into her wedding mantilla for her lover who would not return, as she slowly disappeared through this little door.

This was the same door through which the lover had, only

A basic American urge . . . a door backstage

a scene before, reluctantly exited, promising to return soon (at least in time for the wedding) but, alas, the shattering note arrived instead.

What happened to the señorita and the fine young Spaniard will always be a slight mystery to me. I became lost in the Greek dialogue of the obvious plot. But I do know that, contrary to classical Greek tragedy and Spanish realism, another courier brought another note that seemed to carry glad tidings, and the wedding mantilla was out again.

The National (state-supported) Greek Theater presents classical plays from all countries, as well as revivals of ancient dramas. Both under the same roof—or rather, under the same genius of Rondiris, famous director of the festival plays in Epidaurus, who invited me to the theater where he was rehearsing the chorus of *Agamemnon* for the summer festival.

Mr. Rondiris had a charming sense of humor. When I explained that I had found an off-stage set that intrigued me for photographing, he laughed and said, "You Americans—always something different!" I agreed it was a basic American urge. "But not me," he added; "I create in the tradition." That, I agreed, was a delight and a luxury that few in America could afford, since our theater, like most things, is private enterprise—commercial, and consequently more competitive, requiring constant change and popular appeal. He agreed, and invited me back to the theater.

Orthodoxy and gold-velvet curtains

The Orthodox Greek churches are unpretentious but very handsome, with white classic pillars and gold velvet curtains drawn back before the carved doors.

Behind the doorway of the Papakia (The Little Duck),

Good food and smart people

is Athens' smartest restaurant, opened on a wager by Mrs. Adossides, one of Athens' really unusual women. One room of the tiny restaurant, which is a small house, is decorated in fishing-village style—all very elegant, with fireplaces and hand-woven rugs. It is one of Athens' few good restaurants. Mrs. Adossides was first to organize a sports car rally in Athens and races her own foreign cars. After a beautiful dinner party she drove several guests into the mountains so we could see Athens at night, taking the big Mercedes around the mountain curves like a racing car—and with authority. The Pantheon, though sometimes lighted, this night was black and haunting against the sky. The city sparkled with lights, multiplied along the coast by the sea.

Athens is not like any other city by night or day. Its trains, trams, buses, bicycles, scooters, taxis, seem noiseless as they move through the broad, leafy streets. The tempo is smooth. In most cities life is "jerky": lights on, lights off; cars stop and go, speed up, slow down. Athens glides through the day and night on noiseless hours with less hurry and less neon.

A vine-laden doorway on Mt. Hymettus gives admittance to the beauties of the tenth-century Byzantine church of the Kaisariani Monastery, and at the same time allows the eye

The sweetest honey known

to move over its wall to the cypress-spiraled hills around it, carpeted with green sprinkled with white and yellow field flowers, split with great white rocks, and patched with cerise, pink, purple, and magenta wild anemones. Along the ravines and across the hills the serpentine road is green-walled with cypress.

Here in the famous mountain of honey, among the fig trees and flowers, the bees gather from the hillsides the sweetest honey known.

Inside the monastery walls, the grass is even greener, birds sing from the tall poplars that sigh in the wind, and a meandering waterfall murmurs among the rocks. On the tiny vaulted chapel of the ancient church, built on pagan ruins, is a fine example of the flat, stark, powerful Byzantine painting, lighted by slim candles that burn in brass holders.

We drove back to Athens through the cypress-spired hills and arrived at Floca's for tea, as planned by Mr. Pallis. The pastry was devastatingly delicious. The Greeks are very serious about their tearooms, which are English in their polished, austere atmosphere.

Spiro arrived at the Grande Bretagne the next day (after his day off) at nine o'clock—which is early for Athens—and, via the grapevine of doorman, bellboy, reception desk, and operator, I got the word that my car was waiting. Spiro knew every special view in Athens, every taverna, every twisting street in Piraeus, was aware of where the sun hit at certain times for photography and, within two minutes, how long it took to reach any designated place from any given spot.

From the very top of Piraeus the clean, colorful little houses of the poor look out over Athens, and Lycabettus hill.

These tiny houses drift down the slopes, interwoven with crooked paths, steps, and tiny yards joined together with clotheslines. They have yellow, green, blue, or pink doors and a network of shutters and porches; lean-tos of heavy blue, painted paper; walls patched with shocking-pink tin and propped up with stones and sticks. Dozens of houses were trimmed with blue—that blue that belongs to Greece. Along every road, on every village street, in the shepherds' shacks high on the mountain, all across the islands, a fence, a door, a shutter, a boat: that same incredible blue.

In Piraeus, on the walls of the tavernas, there are traces of the same biue in the mischievously lewd paintings made innocuous by wreaths of flowers, still-like plaster heads of ancient bards, and cherubs mixed among them. There are thousands of tavernas in Athens, and surely 99.9 per cent of them must be in the old city of Piraeus. At twelve o'clock, too early for lunch, we stopped at a taverna for coffee. The small table was covered with a huge plaid, multicolored cloth, soon concealed by the large plate of fish paté made from potatoes and fish, with a dozen black and green olives standing on end in it; a basket of thickly sliced, heavy bread,

made innocent by wreaths of flowers

hot, baked, crisp sardines, and a bottle of Greece's *vin ordinaire,* the spicy Retsina wine that in some way has resin instilled in it. It's indeed heady and, when taken in the context of the taverna, delicious.

At night the tavernas are gay with guitar music and the popular *bousoukia* songs, a mixture of Turkish, Spanish, Greek, and Slavic that's very earthy.

The Taverna Vassilena, famous for its thirty-course hors d'oeuvres, has atmosphere—a stove in the center of the room; old dishcloths stretched from nails across the windows; no furniture except for tables and a counter from behind which these endless tidbits flow by way of the proprietor's family, who serve in a "come just as you are" sort of attire. A list of hors d'oeuvres gives an idea of appetizers found anywhere in Athens. What else is there? One at a time arrives: fried clams, ripe olives, tuna and potatoes, anchovies, raw fish, shredded lettuce, meat loaf, ham, octopus, dolma, hot shrimp balls, small sausage, pastry stuffed with meat, meatballs, sardines, Roquefort and butter, and so on and on.

On another side of Athens, along the sea, an iron doorway opens on streets that zigzag like a ski trail down among fishermen's houses. The harbor of North Faliron, which Athens overlaps, lies far below—a forest of fishing-boat masts. The broad, short street that forms a plaza on the waterfront is lined with cafés and shops and houses. Fishermen spread saffron, brown, orange, and pale blue nets the length of the plaza to dry so that only a narrow strip is left for cars, but this is the fishermen's privilege. Bewhiskered, ancient sea captains sit smoking their pipes, with their pale eyes gazing out to sea. The big awkward brackish-brown and red boats lie in the Greek-blue water like dry brown leaves.

A forest of fishing boats

DOORWAY TO A WORLD,
GREEN AND BLUE AND FAR AWAY

The next day I went to Delphi, where Greece seems nearest to the sky.

Doorway 37, far above the Bay of Corinth on the cypress-spired mountains in Delphi, opens onto a distant painted sea beyond a mirage of mountains.

Through this doorway steps lead down the mountainside, twisting, turning, giving way to a path that criss-crosses down the steep cliff, squeezing past the doors of the tiny square houses braced on their front foundations, holding to the mountainside, clinging to each other, their roofs touching, terracing the steep descent with mottled orange tile.

The houses scatter out quickly as they reach the plateau far below, where sheep and goats graze on lush green grass among patches of yellow flowers. Far below the rocks and cypress a shepherd's shack clings to the quickly descending mountain. Steep foothills and the deep cypress valley are cut across by a silver mountain river that hastens to lose itself in the sea.

Through this door the world is green and blue and far away. On this side runs the sun-bleached mountain-ledge road through Delphi, lined on both sides with whitewashed shops and blue-trimmed houses. Those on the side of No. 37 roost precariously on the cliff that juts out here and there, or on top of the roofs of the houses below. On the other side of the road countless steps climb on up the mountainside through the tiny town of Delphi, white, orange, and blue against the green mountain.

Along the street, chairs sit by the doorways and old men doze. The shop doorways are hung with brilliantly colored, hand-woven wool rugs and embroidery.

Around the curve of the mountain, the road leads to the museum of Delphi, with its treasures of sculpture: the breathtakingly beautiful bronze Charioteer with black-and-white agate eyes—disconcerting eyes, so real that you feel surely the history of the ancients on which he once looked must be registered on the stone retinas of those eyes. Tiny fragments along the eyelids indicate that even eyelashes of metal once made the eyes even more real. With the metal strip of reins still in his hands, the Charioteer stands, as he was unearthed centuries ago, in a small room alone. As the imagination attempts to step back into another world whence the Charioteer came, the beauty of the statue holds the mind here in the little room on the mountaintop.

The ruins of the ancient theater of Delphi lies in the lap of a mountain peak.

The amphitheater's broken and crumbling stones are traced with green and fringed with tiny white flowers pushing up through the crevices. The stones of the stage are outlined in green grass, and fragments of columns lie among the daisies beyond the entrance. Sitting in the white ruins of the theater, looking down endless marble steps and along the pine-canopied walk lost in the green woods, it is easy romantically to repeople this ancient spot. Here on the mountain where Pythia gave her oracles, overlooking the Temple of Apollo, it is easy to believe that one could step through Doorway 37 and vanish into another world.

My last day in Greece was a beautiful, blue and white Greek day. My luggage was in the car. Spiro had arrived, with a huge bouquet of intense purple violets, to take me to the airport, and we were spinning along the edge of the Aegean Sea. I sat quietly, smoking a delicious Greek cigarette.

On arriving in Turkey, I dropped a note to my friend, Becky Stickney Hamilton, Paris editor of London *Harper's Bazaar,* who was leaving Paris soon for a sailing trip through the Greek islands but planned a day in Athens and a trip to Delphi. I suggested she tell the doorman at the Grande Bretagne that she would like to get in touch with Spiro.

Needless to say, this makes me a member in good standing of the Guide Snobs.

Rhodes

DOOR OF "THE PAINTER" OF LINDOS

A WEATHER-BEATEN, unpainted door in the town of Lindos on the Isle of Rhodes is the door of the man called "the painter," who many years ago came as a young man to Lindos, from where no one really knew. He was not Greek, but he spoke Greek; he also spoke and read English and French.

Most doors in Lindos were painted blue or yellow, or the old, dark, paneled wood was preserved with varnish or polish.

Once many years ago, not long after the painter had moved into the house, with easels, cases, paintboxes, rolls of canvas, he started to cover the door with blue paint, but after one corner was covered the strokes of the brush swiped here and there and the lines of a face began to emerge, but the painter never finished. The blue outline sank into the thirsty wood, remained for a few months, and faded.

Always with easel and paints, the young painter was soon seen in the village and along the roads, with his campstool and brushes, and glimpsed in the patio of the house he had bought from the son of an old lady who had died.

The last people to see the house inside, years ago, said it was just as the old lady left it. The floors of the courtyard and the floors inside (with the exception of one room) were —as in every Lindos house—of white pebble mosaic, bordered with patterns of black, with a flower or geometric design in the center. The oval pebbles, about an inch long, set on end in the plaster, look at first glance like a deep, coarse, wool rug.

The family's embroidered pictures were still on the walls. As was the custom in Lindos, a piece of embroidery, depicting figures in a scene of a religious nature or a flowery family tableau, represented members of the family, whose photographed heads were pasted onto the embroidered bodies. The embroidery was covered with glass, and then framed. The old lady's family was well-to-do and there were many of these quaint, beautifully embroidered pieces. The living room, with its fine old divan, china cabinet, stand table, lamps, desk, dark wood chairs, and wide board floors was, like the rest of the house, untouched except for the old woman's bedroom, which was now the painter's studio. But he could never paint in it, for the houses of Lindos have no windows. They stand with one wall serving two houses, shading one another from the blistering sun, getting their light and air from doors onto their courtyards. The house was of the period influenced by the Turkish occupation of Rhodes, and the dining room, except for a narrow space along one side to pass through, was one wall-to-wall wooden platform about the height of a bed, with rugs and pillows spread on it. The family sat cross-legged on the platform and ate from the huge fluted brass Turkish trays. The small bedroom of the house was in the same Turkish manner—a large stage, filling the greater part of the room, where the Turkish families slept en masse. Many of these platforms are left in the Lindos houses and Western beds are set on top of them.

The painter had injected nothing to change the way of living. There were a stone stove and basin in the kitchen. He cared for the flowers in the patio, and every spring, blooming in the pots around the patio, could be seen lilies, enormous yellow dahlias, and sweet-smelling freesias.

The painter, when he was young, sat with the men many afternoons in the taverna across the narrow cobblestone street from the church and drank retsina in the shade of the church tower. As he grew older, he went to the whitewashed church on Sundays when the big bell rang out.

In the Turkish manner

Retsina in the shade of the church

Many stairways to a dark door

When he first came to Lindos so many years ago, the young painter went for many days up the steps that wind through the streets of the village and climbed up past courtyards, houses, shops—up and up, out of the village, and then along the path twisting and circling the mountainous hill, to the walls of the acropolis. He carried his stool and easel and sometimes set them up on the slopes in the shade of the wall, high above the town, where the slopes were a mosaic of red poppies, yellow buttercups, and white daisies, but he rarely, if ever, entered the castle fort. Lindos, one of the three oldest citadels on the island, was very proud of the biggest and oldest acropolis, the site which had been inhabited off and on since before the year 2500 B.C. Many civilizations had come and gone, many stairways had been cut from the solid rock that rose up to the arched, dark, hollow doorway of the castle. Broken and destroyed stairs had to be replaced by new ones cut or built beside them. Statuary had been brought to the rock by one civilization and destroyed by another, but the ruins piled up and new civilizations had built on top of it since the Neolithic period. Sacrifices of all kinds of life had been brought to the goddesses and gods here on the rock.

Inside the fortress castle there are an ancient chapel, a few wall carvings, a passageway, and broad steps that lead to the top of the acropolis. There columns stand, stark and disconnected, scarcely describing a structure, 350 feet above the mottled-blue port of St. Paul, where the water lashes away at the base of the sheer cliff. The defenders of Rhodes for centuries looked out from the acropolis and watched the Aegean Sea for intruders, with an eye on the not-too-distant, hazy shore of Turkey.

Along the other side in the broken wall are turrets which frame the town of Lindos, lying in a valley at the foot of the flowering slope, the flat roofs touching and covered with gray clay to fight off the sun.

. . . like a gray filigree

The painter took long walks through the village and, as years passed, he became familiar to the people of the town. His hair turned gray and then white, just as his door grayed and bleached. He never seemed to want for anything—he always had plenty to eat, to wear, and to paint with, and no one paid much attention to him and his paintings. The people of Lindos were well-to-do or had too much to do to think very much of painting. They were artistic, famous for their colorful Lindos plates, their rugs, and their embroidery, which is their indigenous art. As a matter of fact, no one ever saw the paintings he carried about on squares of wood-edged canvas under his arm.

An eye on the not-too-distant shore

Narrow streets through the village

Every month or so he asked a farmer or a mail carrier to give him a ride into the town of Rhodes, and sometimes he would stay a day or overnight and sketch inside the old walled city. He would sit before the arched gateways of some quaint house, or the market streets with their big prowling cats, or the little blue and white tavernas spilling over the sidewalks.

He would buy special sausage from the sausage shop, wrapped in white muslin, and slices of the huge white cheeses in the cheese stalls, and a bottle of foreign wine.

Along the roads, as the mail carrier or farmer stopped, he would sketch: a woman in a doorway, or cows and sheep nibbling along the rocky coast, or the roses as big as saucers—

A rug of pebbles

the roses from which Rhodes got its name—or the little houses with the four-sided roofs held up by a pillar in the center. As the road, lined with cypress like a green picket wall, curved and wound through the countryside, he said very little. The walls would fall away and the fig orchards would lie over the slopes like a gray filigree, casting tangled, intricate shadows on the grass. A lunch basket would hang in a fig tree with the neck of a wine bottle protruding and a farmer's coat floating from a limb. Sometimes an old olive tree would have a dozen shirts and jackets on its branches as men and women planted tiny white onions in the field. When the orange groves were heavy with big, sweet oranges, he'd ask the driver to stop and he'd pick two. The groves would give way to the orchards of small, bitter oranges good for marmalade, and huge lemons bending the limbs of the lemon trees.

In Rhodes he walked up and down the cobblestone street of the Houses of Languages where, from 1309 to 1522, the Knights of Rhodes each had a house or inn decorated with

Along the road, the painter sketched

his coat of arms. The painter brought back books that told more about the knights who ruled the island for two hundred years; who divided their administrative powers by languages; who chose a Grand Master for life who lived in the Grand Master's castle. There were more French Grand Masters because there were more knights of France, of Provence and of Auvergne, although there were Spanish and Italian knights also.

The painter made a trip, a short one, to Petaloudes (Butterfly Valley), where red and gold butterflies by the thousands fill the ravine from July to September. The trees that attract the butterflies meet in a green canopy over the plunging waterfall that rushes down the ravine, forming cool pools and splashing over the huge stone boulders. Along the sides of the narrow gorge (not much wider than the height of the tallest tree) are paths and footbridges, passing back and forth across the water as the ravine climbs up the mountainside. The effect is of a hall of red and gold and green mosaics, and the constant motion of the butterflies and leaves makes it glitter and shine.

One day the aged painter no longer appeared on the streets, and the neighbor women of Lindos took him food and cared for him. There was no one he wished to write or send for, only afterward the house was to be sold and everything in it as well; the paintings in the studio were all to be burned. His friends did as he said, and the hundreds of canvases stacked to the ceiling were taken out behind the house and burned. One by one, as they were dropped onto the flames, his neighbors saw a woman's face—the same woman's face—on every canvas; no matter where the painting started, it ended with the face—a dark, strong, luminous face, haunting. The tangled branches of the fig trees became her hair; the blue sea, almost finished, turned into her cold blue eyes; the butterflies sketched at Petaloudes were caught in her black hair. Always the canvas started . . . turned into her face . . . and was laid aside. Always trying again——

The brush strokes on the door, long since gone, were the same familiar lines, the beginning of the face.

No letters, no clue, no trace of who the painter was—or whose the face that haunted him.

More French grand masters

Turkey

THE CAREFULLY CLOSED DOOR

51

The shores of the Bosporus—a faint line

ISTANBUL in the misty spring rain was a lovely, mysterious oriental city. The waters of the Bosporus and the Marmara were silver blue, their shores a faint line drawn by the mist. The Golden Horn lay in a dreamy haze, scarcely reflecting the silvered domes and minarets along its banks. The rain turned iridescent on the cobblestone streets that shed the water in a thin stream as they climbed up and down the steep, rocky hills of Istanbul.

Along ancient streets the tiny, unpainted frame houses were silvery gray, and black-eyed children peeped from the lace-curtained windows into the imprisoning rain. Old men and cats took refuge in small coffee houses where the rain pelted against the windows, and the bearded men sat silently smoking huge water pipes on the floor beside them. We, also fleeing the rain, drank small cups of powerful, black, sweet coffee.

At lunch time we escaped from the mist into a gay, bustling restaurant where we dined on yogurt soup, kebab (one of a hundred varieties), eggplant dolmas (one of a thousand dolmas), cold artichokes with oil, and a dessert borek, having started the lunch, of course, with raki (native drink) clouded with water.

The shining domes of Hagia Sophia and Süleymaniye's Mosque rose above the veiled city like silver baubles. The minarets of the great Blue Mosque pierced the low gray sky like six upright swords.

The misty veil over the city returned Istanbul briefly to the mysterious medieval past, making it look perhaps somewhat as it did in its oriental splendor when St. Sophia was a Christian church and the drab old Topkapi Museum was the Grand Seraglio, magnificent palace of the flamboyant sultans of the Ottoman Empire.

The shining dome of Ha

hia

Turkey, unlike many old-world countries, is not a blend of the old and the new. The past has been laid away like a fabulous, outgrown dress of silks and satins, bejeweled and embroidered in gold, handed down through many generations. But with the coming of the Republic, Turkey has donned a new modern dress of its own design and has plunged into a modern, progressive, democratic life, as has no other old-world country. Since the day in 1919 when Mustafa

An old door reopened

Kemal Pasha, known as Atatürk (Father of the Turks) came by the Black Sea to mold the disjointed communities of Turkey into a new world, Turkey has moved away from its past traditions. The intensity with which the Turks devoted themselves to keeping in step with their Western brothers gave them no time or desire to look back, and they find it hard to understand the insistence of foreigners to delve into the colorful past, the barbaric splendor of the once-powerful Ottoman Empire.

But at the Gate of the Executioner, entrance to the enclosure of the Grand Seraglio, the imagination began to badger the mind for clues to the past and tidbits about the drab, medieval Topkapi Palace that held so many treasures from the past and told so little of its almighty sultans who accumulated, hoarded, and lived among its riches—riches that had given such magnificence to the low, rambling stone buildings as to have made the seraglio comparable, in the past, to the palaces of Versailles and Peking and the palaces of the Grand Moguls of India.

The buildings of the seraglio themselves were of little or no importance to the builders, except for the protection and privacy they afforded: they were merely to house the fabulous furnishings of silks, satins, brass, gold, jewels, rugs and tapestries, as the tents of the Seljuk sultans had done for centuries as they swept across the Plains of Anatolia, moving their portable tent-palaces on as they conquered.

The mosaic-decorated walls (which were the only structural decorations) of the old seraglio were intact in the sprawling, secluded harem quarters. But so eager were the Turks to lock off this chapter of the past forever that until recently the harem was closed and every trace of the lives of the black eunuchs and the women of the harem was blotted out.

Beyond this first gate of the old seraglio almost no Turks, and very few from the outside world, had ever passed. And during the centuries few, if any, had left the palace by this gate or any gate. Everyone in the Grand Seraglio was a slave except the Sultan and his children, and the only way out was by way of the bowmen, the chief executioner, or through foul play of other slaves, none of whom were Turks.

Across an unkept park of disorderly trees, the next barrier, the Gate of Happiness, opened into a courtyard directly in front of the Throne Room Without, a small, unimposing building where foreign ambassadors, waiting dignitaries, and royalty (if impressive enough), finally gained admittance to the royal presence. It was here, on a jewel-encrusted rug, deep in diamond-studded pillows, draped in the richest of silks and satins and gold-embroidered velvets, under a ceiling dripping with pearls, that the sultan received the emissaries of the outside world, never speaking to, or looking directly at, the lowly Christians.

Off the gallery that borders one side of the courtyard, doors opened into what is now called the Hall of the Treasury, one of the world's greatest cache of jewels, rare treasures of art, paintings, china, and costumes. Behind the first carefully guarded door was the china pavilion, sheltering the largest collection of Chinese porcelain of the Sung and Yuan dynasties, dating from the ninth to the thirteenth centuries—an incomparable collection of celadon, which was the royal household china used daily in the seraglio and handled by hundreds of slaves. Since it was a crime punishable by death to break a dish, the collection is understandably intact.

The treasury room of clocks is a Rube Goldberg dreamland of solid gold and jeweled clocks of all sizes and description, coveted mainly for their tricks rather than their time telling—golden birds that sing out the time, and a clock in the shape of a tree. Timekeeping in the days of the seraglio was completely unnecessary, for the measurement of time was the muezzins' call to prayer, which the Turks obeyed five times daily, washing their feet and legs to the knees, their

The walls of the mosque —shelter from the rain

All that's left of the splendor

hands and arms to the elbows in the icy water outside the door of the mosques, as they still do in the coldest days of winter at the waterspouts and basins along the old mosque at the doorway of the famous "covered bazaar."

In the Treasury of Jewels is gathered so much splendor cut from emeralds, diamonds, rubies, and every kind of precious stone; so much beauty sculptured from gold and ornamented with pearls; so much exquisite cloth and china shaped into rare beauty that it leaves the eyes bedazzled.

Among the most precious pieces of the collection: an emerald teacup; a three-inch seated figure that is a strangely shaped baroque pearl from the emerald-embedded drapery across the legs to the jeweled headdress; an uncut emerald, several square inches in size, hanging from the pagoda-like roof of a small throne chair. But the most valuable emerald, a large, square-cut stone, rests among the silk and feathers of a sultan's turban in the costume room of the treasury. The stopper of one crystal perfume bottle is mounted with an inch-long baroque pearl.

Masses of rubies, diamonds, pearls, lapis lazuli, crystals, decorate vases, clocks, and objects of art. A crystal coffer two feet long is filled with precious stones of varying sizes, and sits on a jeweled rug as it did when the Sultan received rare guests, members of his court, and his pashas in the Throne Room Within, and from the coffer took a handful of jewels to throw on the floor before them. There are feather fans, each tendril dripping with a diamond, great necklaces, medallions of stone, and gold ankle bracelets that once adorned the favorite ladies of the harem, the harem which now lies bleak and silent off the courtyard across from the treasury.

To reach the harem it was necessary to pass through many guarded doors, the passageway of the quarters of the black eunuchs, or by way of the courtyard of the queen mother, the tyrannical disciplinarian of the 1500 to 2000 women of the harem, who was far more deadly than the eunuchs, who were locked into the tiny cages where they crawled each night after having guarded the harem by day.

Many of the women of the harem were never so much as spoken to by the sultans or ever seen by them, but lived out their entire lives bickering secretly, quarreling in whispers and signs; learning to dance, to embroider, and to play the *saz*. They were given a haphazard tidbit of education. If a woman was even summoned to be looked upon in the sultan's regular review of the harem, she was considered most fortunate, for she might some day see the sultan and become a favorite, or take the place, even, of one of the four unmarried wives who bore his heirs. The harem quarter opened onto two courtyards, one where the women spent much of their time in good weather, and another that led into the stables where the sultan sometimes rode on his silk-swathed horse, clattering over the cobblestones as a treat for the ladies of the harem as he left for the hunt.

The ropes of huge emeralds and diamonds that reside in the treasury, so a British visitor once reported, were worn by the wives of the sultan.

Jeweled swords, sheaths, daggers, holsters, belts, shields, and gauntlets filled cases and covered walls of the treasury. There were other rooms of robes and cloaks and turbans of the sultans, who were absolute rulers. The court, the Janizaries (private army), and members of the Divan (ruling body) were all servants. No one in the palace except the sultan spoke above a whisper, on penalty of death, and hundreds of deaf-mutes functioned importantly.

The emerald-studded, solid-gold throne of Shah Ismail glows and glitters in the halls of the treasury. Even the fabulous throne was in the form of a large settee, barren without its array of jewel-encrusted satin pillows and its richly patterned, gem-dusted rug.

Portraits of many of the proud sultans hint at little secrets of the succession of absolute monarchs who for centuries held a large part of the world in their power as surely as they did the slaves of the seraglio—Suleiman the Magnificent, who broke tradition and married his favorite, Roxelana; Ibrahim, who built a kiosk of sables and bejeweled his beard; Murad IV, who enforced prohibition to a killing degree; Ahmed I, architect of the tortuous *Cage,* a small house where he imprisoned his half-witted brother instead of disposing of him, thus breaking the centuries-old law of fratricide, which had solved the problem of competition for the throne; Mohammed III, who cheerfully destroyed his nineteen brothers; Mohammed II, conqueror of Constantinople; Selim III, one of the many sultans murdered by his fierce Janizaries; Ahmed III, who was a talented gardener and

Another palace on the Bosporus

imported tulip bulbs from Venice and other parts of the world and gave great tulip festivals in the palace at tulip time; and Selim I, (the Grim) who cut off his viziers's heads for eight consecutive years.

Through the centuries, only a few sultans ever appeared outside the seraglio, and then it was required that subjects fall to the ground on their faces at their approach, so almost no one ever saw the exalted rulers. On occasion they drifted briefly on the Marmara Sea, far below the seraglio, in royal caiques.

But all that is left of this splendor is in the Halls of the Treasury.

Another palace still reflects its splendor in the waters of the Bosporus: the Palace of Dolmabahçe, whose great lacy wrought-iron gates open onto the straits of the Bosporus where the royal yachts of the last sultans were anchored, and where today black freighters and big steamers ply the waters, carrying Turkish goods all over the world.

This formal, white palace is akin in some inexplicable way to Versailles. The sultans of Dolmabahçe Palace were much further removed from the tents of Anatolia than the builders of the seraglio, and architecture had taken on significance. The palace lies gently, endlessly, along the water, with a high stone wall hiding it from the other three sides. Here Atatürk passed his last days, in Room 71, the smallest and most simply furnished of all the hundreds of elaborate rooms, which are still furnished as they were then, with the priceless objects of art, clocks, rugs, chandeliers, tapestries, curtains, and treasures of bric-a-brac. The grand staircase is surely one of the richest in existence.

Not far away, the three towers of the fortress-castle of Rumelihisar, with its iron-studded doors, rise on the banks of the Bosporus, built by Mehmet II two years before the conquest of Istanbul and completed, so it is said, in three months. Beside the main fortress towers (which have lost their cone roofs), many small ones scale the steep hill from which a watch could be kept across the straits to Asia and along the coast of the Marmara Sea.

On the highest hill above the straits, the Istanbul Hilton's modern balconies and glass façade look out over the interlac-

Black freighters pass the lacy gates

A watch across the straits

ing of the Black Sea, the Marmara Sea, the Bosporus, and the Golden Horn that cuts Istanbul in two, leaving part of the city in Asia and part in Europe—the only city astride two continents. Much of the gay life of Istanbul centers here in the lush dining rooms and night clubs. At tea-dance time, the whole, vast dining room and lobby are overflowing with smartly dressed Turkish men and women. The seraglio, just across the Golden Horn, seems so far away—did it really exist at all?

A hill rises in the distance and turns from a hazy outline to yellow, orange, and red, painted with the tile roofs of the small houses that cover every inch of the hill. The old walled city of Ankara can be entered only on foot. Inside the walls are narrow streets, wandering clay pathways, small courtyards among the houses of the poor, some of which have scaled the great stone wall of the city and are partly perched on top of it.

At the bottom of the old city begins new Ankara, capital city of the Turkish Republic, with broad streets, modern buildings, and parks that scatter over the surrounding hills. A city built in twenty years but already the home of the National Theatre, the State Opera, universities, and important museums, Ankara is a small, gay city. At a dinner party at the Palas Pavillon, an Italian orchestra played cha-chas and sambas, and every man in the dinner party was an excellent dancer and every woman was beautifully dressed and attractive.

The women of Turkey are particularly surprising. In their new-found freedom, they are quietly and gracefully taking their places in many fields. I met women judges, teachers, radio personalities, and women in the professions and in business—even high in the government. Nowhere are women held in higher esteem. This dream of Atatürk's has surely come to realization long before even he could have hoped.

The hospitable pink mansion of Turkey's charming President Bayar stands on a high hill surrounded by gardens, where his enchanting granddaughters in pink dresses and pony tails picked carnations from the garden for me when tea was over.

Houses on the old Ankara wall

A CAPRICE OF NATURE ON THE PLAINS OF ANATOLIA

In Kayseri, Anatolia, (once the capital of Cappadocia), Christianity was practiced as early as the first century in grottoes in great secrecy, which may account for the solitary rock churches of the Valley of Göreme. But no one really knows the history of the Fairy-Chimney churches. Hundreds of the strange yellow cones with flat rocks balanced on their peaks are clustered together in groups and rows among rocks and scraggly bushes—geological wonders formed by Nature in some inconceivable way. Some of the Fairy Chimneys can be entered by crawling through dark passages; or, some have a maze of holes and tunnels by which you can ascend to the top of the rock. Throughout these dim sanctuaries is a feeling of security and peace. Outside, the ground, the dust, the stone are yellow and arid, the sun bright, and the heat intense in the valley where a sluggish yellow river, half water, half flowing clay, moves languidly among the grotesque rocks.

Were the smooth, sculptured cones the work of a raging torrent dwindled to the stream that now trickles through the bewitched valley? What freak of nature formed the stalagmite world of rock sanctuaries today in various stages of ruin, turning the valley into a Dali fantasy? Tiny galleries inside are half broken away. Whole sides of some cones have dropped away and left the interior showing like a child's drawing of a house where you see through the walls, exposing the small chambers in which the monks lived, with their stoves, wine presses, and chapels.

In this grotesque village of rupestrian churches is Karanlik Kilise (the dark church), where a tunnel opens in the base of the rock, shadowy paintings on the walls are indistinct, and the atmosphere is gloomy and heavy. On the walls of Tokali church are depicted stories of the New Testament. The liturgical furniture is as it was left. All that is really known is that a caprice of nature created the yellow stone Fairy Chimneys, and men, for spiritual freedom, hollowed them out and imprisoned themselves for shelter.

Egypt

DOOR TO THE DESERT

From this jagged doorway in the side of Cheops's Pyramid at Giza came secrets of Egypt's past, given up by the desert reluctantly, as is every tomb, every stone and grain of sand that is wrested from the vast, greedy Sahara.

Aided by the constant sun and the ceaseless winds, the sands reach out over the limestone pyramids, once covered with impenetrable granite which the flaying sands and molesters have long ago torn away. Only a small patch of the grayish-red granite at the peak of the tomb remains, leaving the golden limestone piled into steps from base to top.

The sand ocean flows around the scattered palms of the desert and, as for centuries, piles up against the great temples of Abu Simbel, the Colossi of Memnon, and the Pyramids of Giza along the Nile.

The desert does not sleep. It's ever watchful: moving, shifting, begrudging the smallest oasis its drops of water. It slithers down to the very banks of the Nile, sifts across the Nile Delta, and settles on the shores of the Mediterranean, taking back each day every inch of sand the blue tides swallow. It lies humped up into dunes sprawled out into valleys, and ripples in waves around the pyramids, watching the ever-expanding desert city of Cairo encroaching on its vast wastes.

A gaping door in the side of the ancient tomb leads up a steep tunnel of worn, chipped steps cut from the stone. The passageway, filled with shadow and not tall enough to stand in, ascends past black holes a hundred feet deep, once filled with treasures, along caverns and the chambers where Cheops rested with his queen for thousands of years undisturbed, no doubt thinking that they would be safe until they embarked in their solar ships to begin another fabulous life.

Only the chamber of Cheops himself, halfway up the 450-foot stone pyramid, retains its sarcophagus. The tomb's treasures of relics—jewels, ivory-inlaid chests, chairs, bowls, art, and the mysteriously mummified bodies wrapped and painted with their portraits—are now labeled and displayed in the Egyptian Museum in Cairo, relics astounding the world with their prophecies of science, art, engineering, and medicine.

From inside the dark passage of the pyramid, the jagged door frames Cairo, lying in the sun, fringed with green gardens, fields, and trees, a golden-beige alabaster city criss-crossed with rows of palms. Slim minarets rise above the limestone buildings—buildings all white and beige, like drifts of sand among the palms on the banks of the green Nile. Trees cut in the shape of upside-down fezzes border the streets.

Lying before the pyramids at Giza, the Sphinx faces the Nile, with its back to the desert where a new, straggling tent city dots the sand—Sahara City: a gambling casino; a huge tent restaurant where dinner is served on large brass tray-tables to guests on low couches while famous belly dancers, costumed in a few strings of beads, perform the authentic, unexpurgated oriental dances.

Beyond these straggling tents is the sand, the sun, the wind—the Sahara, that scorches intruders by day and freezes them at night in the vacuum of the desert, which has no smell, nothing to touch, no sound.

Pushing back the desert on both sides of the river, Cairo is a growing modern city of broad streets, where the winds blow hot and dry, small apartment houses, elegant town houses, modern hotels, fine restaurants and night clubs.

A jagged door frames Cairo

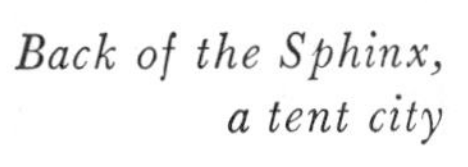

Back of the Sphinx,
a tent city

Across a gangplank, through an Arabian curtained door, is the Omar Khayyam Restaurant, anchored in the Nile. Inside, the dark, wood-paneled walls, brass bowls and braziers gleam in the candlelight. Fluted brass trays a yard across are the tables in the small, first-deck dining room. Above is the bar. The food is excellent, the drinks right. From cocktails on, it's abuzz. The creamy buildings of Cairo, the palms, and the stars are mirrored in the water of the Nile that laps the sides of the boat.

Ex-king Farouk's ex-yacht, anchored along the opposite bank, is now a smart restaurant-night club.

Behind the doors of Club Fontana, overhanging the banks of the Nile, is, I'm sure, the only belly dancer in the world who dances in the once-fashionable sack—a gray sheath from neck to ankle, slit modestly to the knee on either side. Over it, a much-beaded, fringed hip-band shimmers and defines the exotic movements of the hips of the dancer, who scarcely moves her feet during the half hour of continuous dance. One of the most famous dancers of Egypt, she dances to a panting crowd each night. She has putty-colored hair and wears a quizzically bland smile during the entire performance, which somehow heightens the hypnotic spell of the sensual dance. Occasionally the light picks up her figure through the sheath, but for the most part, as she writhes and quivers, the fringe traces the intricate gyrations, and the whole movement of the dance is effectively suggested through the shapeless sheath.

The new Nile Hilton would make the ancient Pharaohs' eyes sparkle. One side, all mosaic, faces the main plaza in the city. The other side mirrors its balconies in the Nile. Modern Egyptian décor tastefully bejewels the truly fabulous dining rooms, bars, night clubs, and ballrooms which the Egyptians have taken to their hearts. The service would please even King Tut.

Cairo is a gay city and, like the desert, never sleeps, except with one eye open during the heat of the day. Many people arrive at their offices at ten A.M. and leave them by three for lunch, often for the day. Others are back at work from five to eight. Dinner is at eleven o'clock, and the cabarets begin when the restaurants close at one.

The Pharaohs' eyes would sparkle

Through a doorway on the Nile

About three A.M. Cairo drifts home, when the cool, dry breeze is stirring the palm leaves and the minarets of Mohammed Ali's alabaster mosque overlooking the city are still silhouetted against the sky. One of the world's most beautiful mosques, the interior is all golden alabaster, paneled in a hundred different designs of the gold and white transparent stone, which the sun lights up as it slants through the windows and falls on the rich oriental rugs. Its gardens are high on the rocks of the citadel above the city.

Along the sun-baked streets of Cairo are small sidewalk restaurants with two or three spotlessly clean tables framing the doorways, invitingly set with starched napkins that stand like pyramids, and pink and red flowers in Egyptian pottery bowls. Inevitably a tattooed lamb, covered in red and blue designs from where its head was to where its feet were, hangs on an iron hook outside the door.

Children play on the steps of a small, half-hidden Moslem temple, and black goats forage along the sidewalks.

High, two-wheeled narrow carts, like hayracks, clatter along the street with ten or fifteen women and girls perched on them like roosting birds. They are dressed in black, flounced Mother Hubbards and black scarves to keep off the sun and the wind. They are from the country and on their way to old Cairo, where the Khan al-Khalil bazaars line the maze of narrow streets; where goats and cats wander among the crowds of Arabs wearing fezzes and flowing robes, with argyle socks and Western shoes peeking from under them.

Some of the little stalls and shops are like ships—there's more hidden below the surface than shows above. Down a flight of stairs, the 8 × 10 Lucky Bazaar, (with its proprietor having his smoke outside), turns into an emporium of rooms filled with hassocks, men's silk robes, alabaster old and new, rugs, and gold jewelry.

Fabric shops fill a dozen streets; tailors run their vintage machines at top speed; belabored hand printing presses clatter; barbers cut hair; and real gold jewelry is displayed—all in open stalls along the same street.

At the opera in Ataba Square, Cairo's smart crowds gather for an opening night. Taxis, Rolls-Royces, and old

Starched napkins and tattooed lam

In a street doorway

Egyptian robes . . . argyle socks

Distinguished though unpretentious

Packards squeeze through the gates of the wrought-iron fence that surrounds it. Through its curtained portico pass Cairo's beautifully dressed women, in clothes from Paris and the smart shops on Soliman Pasha, the Fifth Avenue of Cairo. Women of Egypt have, to a marked degree, the fatal beauty long ago attributed to Cleopatra. They apply make-up boldly and jewels with abandon. They have the "it" look of the Italian women, wear clothes with the savoir-faire of the French, and, unlike American women, are not afraid to look glamorous.

The Opera itself is more than just a structure; it is the acceptance of a challenge and significant of the character of the Egyptians. Under Khedive Ismail, European monarchs were invited to visit Cairo. It was suddenly decided that the old opera house was much too shabby to receive the royal guests—so in three months a distinguished, though unpretentious, new one was completed to the satisfaction of all concerned, somewhat of a marvel and a clue to how the pyramids were tackled by their ancestors.

When the sun beats down on Ataba Square and the heat rises from the stones of al-Tahrir Plaza, Cairo's social and well to do move en masse down the green Nile to the beaches and casinos of Alexandria, where life takes on some of the color and gaiety of the days of the seemingly forgotten Cleopatra. The site of the glorious Egyptian queen's palace by the sea is now occupied by the Trion tearoom and goes unmarked except by the pointing finger of a guide. The obelisk that proudly stood at the palace gate now decorates New York's Central Park and the spot on which it stood is an unnoted alleyway.

Though many F's have been removed from doorways and gates of the palaces of Alexandria recently occupied by ex-king Farouk, the unsurpassed lavishness of his domicile on the Egyptian Riviera is still in evidence.

Over the main door to Montazah Palace, F is still a part of the design, though the grounds are open to the public as a sightseeing and resort area. The playing field of the young princes is now a small dog-racing track, the bathhouse a lunch terrace surrounded by orange groves, battalions of palm trees, hedges, and flowers, vistas and drives.

The sprawling three-hundred-room palace Ras-el-Tin, where King Farouk said farewell to Egypt, stretches its esplanades like long white arms along the sea in an embrace. Its gardens are exquisite, and dozens of kiosks of singing birds are scattered through them. Only a few years ago, on a moonlit night, the yacht Mahrousa lay in the harbor nearby, waiting to take the last of the Egyptian kings forever from the sands of Egypt.

Here the Sahara and the Mediterranean "lay on" one of the Middle East's great displays of beach, along the slow curve from the wall of the palace of Montazah the full length of Alexandria, dotted with cabañas and umbrellas. Built out over the Mediterranean are dozens of casinos that keep the night life late and gay.

By the desert road at night, Alexandria is only a three-hour drive at most. Nothing but bramble, sand, and a concrete line straight across the desert for two hundred miles.

Along the delta road that winds and twists to keep in touch with the Nile, a hatmaker's shop is a shade cooler inside than outside, where the felt hats are drying on a rack in the parching sun and wind. Inside, stacks of fezzes wait to be molded on the wooden blocks.

The Moslem farmer is never without his tasseled fez: in the fields with his oxen, breaking up the dry clods with a crude wooden harrow; along the roads, barefoot, with his camel or donkey, his head is always covered with the tapered felt hat.

Farid, the hatmaker, sits cross-legged on a rug. Above him on the wall are four pictures that tell the story of his life and the lives of thousands of Egyptians like him: one a photograph of a house—his home; one, in a gilt frame, of a man in uniform—his country's leader; one a painting of a mosque—his religion; and one a fragment of Egyptian script, which may well have been the poetry of Omar Khayyam or, as easily, his business license. His long scarf hangs on a peg and his blocks, pail, and molds are around him. The straw on the roof overhangs and shades the doorway.

This day, Farid must go to the nearby town to buy felt and meager supplies for his household.

When the sun begins to drop, the felts on the rack have dried and are set inside. The hatmaker's wife has piled cucumbers, maize, and berseem in the tall basket she balances on her head. His son is dressed in his best robe. The camel has been fed, and they start, barefoot, along the dusty road, the wife in her black cotton Mother Hubbard, flounced at the hem, and her black shawl; brass hoops dangling from her ears and bracelets flashing around her ankles. On one hip she carries a baby wrapped in a strip of flowered cotton.

The weekly trip to the village is very exciting for Farid's wife and his son, who work hard in the small field day after day. Another small son is perched on his father's shoulder. They pass the scattered houses of their friends, who wave from the fields. Other farmers along the way are gathering tall grass for their donkeys. Other women in black Mother

The hatmaker along the delta

Hubbards along the road balance brass jugs of water on their heads for the men working in the fields.

The towering palms, with fronds like feather dusters, reaching up and growing high, offer no shade from the still-hot sun, but the little caravan rests under a gnarled olive tree and drinks cool water from the jug tied to the camel's saddle.

They pass the beekeeper's doorway that leads up a ladder onto the flat roof of his mud plaster house where the bees nest in the mud hives and, feeding on dates and delta flowers, produce strange desert honey.

As the farmer's family enters the village other farmers join them. More women in black dresses with huge dried cakes of camel dung and straw, to be sold for fuel, stacked high on their heads. Crowds are gathered around the mosque, and the village shops look gay indeed to Farid and his family as

the oil lamps are lighted and the streets and sidewalk restaurants fill with villagers.

Long after the sun has left the pale desert sky, they trudge back along the road. The night is black, though the sky is splattered with stars. The heat of the day has drifted away, leaving the Nile valley cool, as the hatmaker and his family move silently along the roadside. Young Farid has bought out the shops with his eyes and has drunk a Pepsi-Cola. His wife is happy with her new cloth and an anklet for her small

The poorest house—a carved door

daughter. The hatmaker has bargained well and his camel is laden with bags of grain, spice, and felt for new fezzes.

The doors of the scattered houses, outlined faintly against the sky, are only black holes; unseen dogs growl as the slow steps of the camel on the packed dirt punctuate the still night. The desert sky turns from black to blue, and soon into a white-hot desert day.

Along the delta road are many scattered brick and plaster farmhouses like Farid's, with straw insulating the roof, under which the camel lies in his stall next to the family. But in the poorest house the wooden doors are beautifully, though crudely, carved, and paneled handsomely enough for a town house in Alexandria or Cairo. Every man, even the poorest peasant, in his desire to express his love of beauty, uses his door to speak for him—to set his home apart.

Smokers in a roadside coffee house

In the distance, many huge white sails zigzag across the flat delta among the palm trees, like a mirage, as they coax flat boats through the small tributaries of the Nile and canals cut across the delta into the desert. Flat bridges over the streams loom suddenly in the road.

Low mud houses cluster around one of the canal bridges. In a wide space in the canal on the desert side of the bridge three of the barges lie with their sails dropped, waiting to be relieved of their cargo of sand, grain, seed, and bulging sacks of cotton.

Standing at the approach to the small bridge, I had fitted the boats neatly into my Rolleiflex viewer when an engaging voice said, "Welcome to Egypt." I thought I had not seen, but heard, a mirage. I involuntarily pressed the shutter as I turned to the voice behind me, taking a panoramic view of half of Egypt. A tall (most Egyptians are), handsome (most Egyptians are), man in Western clothes extended his hand and I accepted it.

In excellent English he asked about the camera and talked charmingly on the different techniques of photography. From where had this gentleman dropped, here on a side road between Cairo and Alexandria—had he flown in on a jet camel or dropped from a palm tree? He certainly hadn't come out of one of those straw-topped houses. He may have had a few questions in his mind, too—a woman standing in the above-described spot with a camera, alone.

We walked down the road to where my car and driver (no English spoken here) were waiting. At the car he said, "I'm terribly sorry, but did you get the picture?" I said not unless I had the camera set at panorama 1/8000ths of a second by some chance.

He laughed and said, "It's forbidden to take pictures of any bridges in certain parts of Egypt."

I assured him I was no candidate for jail on the picture I'd gotten. He inquired whether I was on my way to Alexandria, and explained he was a government official and an engineer on an inspection of the dam just completed and other nautical projects nearby. His destination was his headquarters a few miles on, but he lacked a car to return, since he had had a ride this way.

I invited him to be my guest, the driver beamed, and a very pleasant half hour later we crossed a new bridge. Along the elevated road approaching it was a small plateau of ground a few steps down, on which was a quaint, small, two-story building, very old, with a porch on the second floor.

A flower garden in full bloom filled the plateau beside the Nile. This was Mr. Faridez's headquarters.

We were served coffee here by his servant on a small table under a fig tree, where we were soon joined by some fifteen other engineers—many of whom would have attracted favorable attention on Madison Avenue—and workers who as they were introduced, smiled and formed a pleasant circle around us without saying a word. I took their picture in a group, which amused and pleased them, and they cut down half the flower garden for me when I left. The car was one big bouquet of red, blue, white, and pink petunias, stock, and sweet william.

This is typical of Egypt's politeness, humor, charm, and adroitness in the use of co-operation between people. This patient and oblique approach is evident on every level of negotiation involving the smallest and briefest contact.

Sails out of the desert

Lebanon

FOUR THOUSAND YEARS THROUGH A DOORWAY

IN THE tiny country of Lebanon, overlooking the Mediterranean, a doorway beneath a chapel leads to the twelfth-thirteenth-century castle of the Crusaders in the ancient city of Byblos, the oldest continuously inhabited city known. The doorway stands intact, and remnants of the wall in varying stages of decay still support the chapel and a half dozen of the old barlongue towers.

Small houses embedded in sections of these crumbling ramparts use them for one wall, occasionally with windows tunneled through the walls, which may have second stories boosted upon them.

Other parts of the wall are hidden among banana groves and overhung with olive trees. Grass and vines have grown over the ramparts. Just inside the once-impregnable doorway, which stands on a narrow street among the souks, spreading palms and white houses, is a courtyard which was once the approach to the castle drawbridge, long ago replaced with a bridge of rough stones.

An ancient wooden door leads into the castle of the Crusaders di Embriaci of Genoa, Lords of Gibelet within the country of Tripoli, who ruled Byblos (Jebail) for eight generations. The oldest Crusader castle in Lebanon, Syria, or Palestine, Byblos is the last castle of Lebanon to be abandoned by the Crusaders. It shows signs of Roman masonry in the surrounding ruins of thousands of years B.C.

Huge granite columns embedded in the massive stone walls of the donjon (dungeon) are believed to have been taken from the ancient temple of Adonis. The entire underground area of the castle forms a perfectly preserved cistern for withstanding prolonged sieges.

The moat is still very much in evidence, bridged at the entrance with an arched Mameluke cobblestone bridge, which was an addition of the fourteenth century. The original stone stairway of the castle has been cleared and now goes from the dungeon up two flights to "the keep."

. . . like a map to be read

In the remaining walls are arrow turrets, long slits in the stone three inches wide, through which arrows could be shot. The standing walls retain a cannon ball lodged there during the British invasion of 1840. Their defeat resulted in the fall of the Prince of Lebanon and his Egyptian forces, which threw Byblos and Lebanon back under Turkish rule.

Strangely enough, the tombs of the Crusader family of Embriaci have never been found in or around or under the castle, nor in the nearby twelfth-century Crusader Cathedral of St. John the Baptist.

Surrounding the castle on the slopes along the Mediterranean are the ruins of 7000 years of civilization, laid out like a map to be read.

There are even traces of the prehistoric Stone Age, marked Neolithic and Chalcolithic sites, with remnants of the white crushed limestone floors of the dwellings of five to seven thousand years ago. There are shallow graves beneath them, the undisturbed bones indicating the occupants were buried in the embryonic position. The Chalcolithic burial grounds spread over the Neolithic grounds across the acropolis and beyond, their dead encased in large jars and supplied with food, water, gold, knives, jewelry, and pottery to use in the life hereafter.

Civilization piled on civilization leaves something of each. Here is the royal well or spring that is believed to have attracted the prehistoric people to the site that is now Byblos.

Between 3000 and 2150 B.C., as the copper and bronze age passed, Byblos became a well-known city-state, active in foreign trade and with strongly established cultural relations with Egypt. The history of Byblos of this period is written in the ruins of the temples of Baalat Gebal and Reshef, on the ruins of which successive religious structures were built for the next 3000 years. The site of these temples became holy ground. On this historical map of stones and grass drawn by Time on the earth's face, massive stone steps now leading nowhere, circular cisterns, broken walls, stone carvings, tell the story of this long-ago civilization.

The Phoenician ramparts of another time are now overgrown with grass and crumbling at the edge of the water, which wears away at them.

The next period of Byblos' history is told by the Tomb of Kings from the nineteenth to the eighteenth centuries B.C. These tombs contained gifts from the twelfth dynasty Pharaoh, Amenemhat III, to Abishmou I, earliest reigning prince of Byblos. This tomb is entered by stone stairs and through a solid-rock tunnel where one of the sarcophagi of the royal family still remains. The burial wells were a marvel of ingenuity. First the wells were filled with sand, then the huge stone sarcophagus was placed on the sand. As the sand was slowly removed from the deep well, the great stone sarcophagus lowered itself safely to the bottom. And who, thought these clever ancients, could raise it to the surface again to pry into its sacred remains? Beside this foolproof tomb they inscribed warnings to beware of disturbing the royal dead.

On another slope, a piece of the Hyskos wall remains.

From the centuries between 1580 and 734 B.C., the beginning of the Iron Age, scant inscriptions on and from the royal tombs and fragmentary structures are the only remains from the period of the Egyptian suzerainty and Phoenician independence. Some of these Phoenician inscriptions are among the earliest known to history.

The time of Mesopotamia and Persian rule, 734 to 332 B.C., is told by pillars and the King's Dedication Tablet, and from this civilization the first coins ever to be used as currency were found.

The Greeks and the Romans left colonnades; a beautiful amphitheater with the blue backdrop of the Mediterranean behind a raised white stone stage; an acropolis; sections of granite columns; fragments of cornices; and the outline of a vast Roman temple enclosure supposedly dedicated to Adonis, where for hundreds of years the Greek orgies in memory of Adonis were held, during which women gave themselves to strangers indiscriminately for one day of the year.

Started in 1115 A.D., the Crusaders Cathedral was built for the Latin Bishops of Gibelet, dedicated to St. John the Baptist, and still stands in a remarkable state of preservation. Then came the Crusaders di Embriaci and "This is where we came in" on this 7000-year continuous historical show on the hillsides of Byblos.

Touching the town on the other side, the castle looks out over Byblos—the souks (markets), arcaded streets, banana groves, palms, and little white houses. Along the road to Beirut, amber-colored sheep graze on the clay hills; bottle-green cedars stand guard at the doors of a little white church overhanging the sea, with the cross silhouetted against the blue water.

Seen through an unfinished stone archway, Beirut juts out into the sea. Lebanon, a strip one hundred and twenty miles by thirty miles of clay, sand, and rock, is dotted with towns clinging to the blue sea to get away from the scorching breath of the desert beyond the hills. At their backs is the narrow valley, a brush stroke of gray-green olive trees against the purple hills that rise immediately into the snowy Lebanon mountains.

Not to be outdone by the Egyptians, Nature created here her own colossi: the Cedars of Lebanon. It took one thousand to fifteen hundred years for them to reach their present size; some of these four hundred giants that still stand in the snows at Jebel Makhmal are forty feet in circumference. The Egyptians once hauled them away to whittle them into solar-ships.

Beirut is cut out of the sand and stacked on a clay hill, a new city with modern apartment buildings everywhere, new hotels, night clubs, restaurants, and shops smothering the old city. A forest park of small cedars cut (or perhaps they grow that way) like round lollypops on sticks. They are also stuck all along the streets very decoratively.

The architecture is extremely modern. Sometimes an attempt at oriental flavor is injected into a door of modern mosaic and metal.

Behind the mountains that frame the city is the Arabian desert. At the city's feet is the Mediterranean, and overhead is an invisible gateway in the sky, with continuous planes, from the smallest to the big Pan American Clipper Jets, funneling in from the orient to Beirut and fanning out over the Mediterranean to Africa, Europe, and the West.

The castle looks out over Byblos

Cedars guard a chapel by the sea

Nepal

THE GREEN DOOR OF KATHMANDU

ALONG the dark gallery, great white arches are thrown to the stone floor by the moonlight, and a pattern of lace follows the balcony rail the full length of the old palace.

A scattering of dimly lighted windows on the second floor are the only marks on the pure black-and-white night of Kathmandu. Not only the town, but the whole silver-plated Kathmandu Valley lies shining against the sky halfway up the Himalayas.

Some say that centuries ago, when the valley was a mountain lake, it was the home of the moon, and that the moon still rises out of the valley to overflow the rim of the surrounding mountains and light the rest of the world. On nights like this the old palace takes on an elegance of days when it was a rana palace, before it became Nepal's finest hotel. At one end of the hotel the pillars of the gallery are halted by a small wing set even with the columns along the front.

In the shadows where the wing joins the gallery an occasional sliver of light breaks the darkness as a small green door opens and closes. A glow of firelight lights up the red curtains hung inside against the cold that would enter and the warmth that might leave with the shadowy figures that come and go.

Behind this small door is the most remote cosmopolitan bar in the Far East. It's filled with mystery and, at the same time, has a paradoxical naïve quality of the East.

Here Nepal's handful of society, politicians, and royalty mix with strangers who have come from very far for many reasons. For those escaping from a world of too many people, it's quiet and concealing; for those escaping from a world of too few people, it's warm and enveloping. For those who come just for a drink, there is a choice of scotch, sherry, or brandy, and they get it from the old, dark, wooden bar themselves.

The buzz of many subdued voices fills the room with many languages. The red curtain at the door reflects the open fire that burns in the center of the room, like a campfire, on a low, round stone platform that takes up the greater part of the room. Above the fire is a huge brass funnel chimney that disappears in the darkness above the low flames.

Around the fire is a solid ring of chairs, and on the stone platform rest slim Italian pumps; overshined British oxfords; casual American moccasins; square-toed, rubber-soled Polish and German travel shoes; sexless, English gentlewomen's walking shoes; an Indian sandal half hidden by a gilt-bordered sari, and a pair of very old tennis shoes, mixed among other leather-clad feet, worn and worldly, new and nondescript.

An occasional break in the circle leaves a briefly vacant chair.

In the shadowy room, lighted only by the fire and candles on the bar, faces glow and eyes flash. Back of the circle, at the edge of the fire, other figures move about or sit indistinguishable in a second row of chairs around the wall. The flickering firelight gives a sameness to the figures in the room, as the moonlight outside gives a oneness to the gray-shawled natives huddling around their smoldering fires.

The buzz of conversation is broken imperceptibly by leave-takers and arrivals through the red curtains that are pulled aside by a bearer in his native white tunic and cap.

A brilliantly jeweled woman in a sari is framed against the red curtain. Her black eyes search the room. Behind her, a man stands tall again as he emerges from the little door.

A group of young men at the bar encircles a Junoesque girl, with blond hair almost to her waist, who is gracefully smoking a long black cigar, which she puffs as she gazes dreamily into the fire.

Here royalty comes to breathe some good stale air as a change from an endless, drafty, four-hundred-room palace. A young prince comes to be among his friends on returning from the States to find his brother, the king, adamantly objecting to his on-again off-again romance. His friends close around him and speak with real affection in their Nepalese-Oxford voices.

The moonlight gives a oneness

Doors less than five feet high

An American diplomat and his wife and a royal uncle of the prince take places in the circle just vacated by three British foreign correspondents. Nepalese Army brass at the bar talks with the proprietor, a huge sad Russian.

Groups shift from the chairs to the bar, the back row to the front, and conversation shifts from politics and love to tennis. A slim young man, Nepal's tennis champion, Shail Kumar, moves to bow to his young prince, who puts his arm across his shoulder and asks for a game of tennis. The tennis date is made for six A.M. and is immediately nullified by plans for a late supper party for the prince. Looking and acting very American after many months in the States, the prince hugs his friends or gives them a clap on the back.

Wood is added to the fire, glasses refilled, and talk grows more animated and more intimate. Unofficial comments are passed off in loud, confidential whispers.

A French countess and the Polish foreign correspondent leave together.

USOM and USIS (U. S. Government agencies), from up on the hill where they live it up in an old palace, tangle red tape a little tighter and stretch a project for another six months while they complain volubly of the hardships of living in this top-of-the-world paradise. The wives talk of their husbands' civil service rank, and agree that they should be able to buy cars and Nepalese antiques at the PX as they do everything else.

A raja and a shooting American novelist and their Nepalese host talk over tomorrow's tiger hunt that's being laid on in the mountains near Assam, for which they'll leave at dawn with their beaters and their bearers, their chefs and their orderlies, to shoot in the fathomless forests of Nepal, where the sound of a gun is rarely heard and the name of the late Jim Corbett is not used to scare little tigers. These perpendicular forests and plateaus belong to the tiger, the deer, the boar, the lion, and the birds, and to the masses of wild flowers that in spring grow bold and spread out of the forest to cover the hillsides and the Valley of Kathmandu.

There is in this little room a feeling of suspended time, a moment in space where everything is standing still waiting for the parting of the red curtains and for the figures in the room to step back reluctantly through the green door.

Outside the green door is Kathmandu. The courtyard of the old hotel is as light as noon, and beside an occasional door a bearer is huddled in his white shawl, defined by his black moon-shadow that breaks the white wall. Everything is still except the discordant notes from the one-stringed sarangi that is carried on the night air for a moment, then is lost. Not far away, on the main street of Kathmandu, the one-story white plaster stores and stalls are deserted and transformed into stark patterns of black and white.

Life flows over the temples

Past the gateway of the old town along the mall little clusters of squatting figures hug the fires under the bordering trees. Some have lain down close, for the night is cold and no one will sleep warmly. But here the natives have a feeling of closeness and warmth, for during the day the sun shines warmly on groups of people talking and laughing, and children playing. On festival days parades take place on the grass, and sometimes royal ceremonies and games.

It's warmer outside than inside the damp, dirt-floored houses, and pine-wood smoke rises from the courtyards behind the main street where Kathmandu's thousands of poor live around the market and temples that dominate their simple existence. Through doors less than five feet high, passages lead into dozens of moon-flooded courtyards, each sheltering a small temple, a shrine, a holy stone, a religious symbol, or a god carved from wood and painted and ornamented with brass and mosaics, red-streaked with holy powder and bedecked with ribbons and charms that shine in the bright night. Black-haired children, now sleeping, play around and over them by day, when they aren't squatting at their games of pitching Nepalese coins at squares scratched on the sodden earth that the wind of summer will turn to gray dust.

The pagoda-roofed temples cast shadows down upon their constantly repeated erotic sculpture and carvings, realistically painted in many colors, but the wide ribbons of brass and gilt that overhang the roofs and run to the topmost

Squares scratched on the sodden earth

Lacy carved houses face the square

point, symbolizing the path to heaven, are turned to a silver thread by the moonlight and lost in the sky.

The two-story brick houses turn their lace-trimmed fronts to the courtyard gods—carved wooden eaves, shutters, balconies and whole top floors in intricate patterns of birds, faces of a hundred different gods, animals, and abstract designs. Some of the carvings are old and rotting.

The gray figures sit motionless in the white light before hollow doors in the black-and-white courtyards, watching their fires, turning their heads occasionally toward the temples. Mixed among them, transfixed by the same spell of the quiet night, lie big bony white cows. Dogs shift quietly from a doorway to a shadow out of the wind.

Hundreds of temples are strung zigzag through these few square blocks of the old town. The stalls and shops hover around them, and the market creeps up their steps and into their very doors.

One serpentine passage, wide enough for a pedicab, leads intuitively through courtyards and tiny streets. Along this twisting path unfolds the story of the Nepalese religion, told by the temple carvings, the symbols, and droning, chanting monks before the open balconies. The way starts with a primitive shrine in a sunken spot in the cobblestones, a religious symbol surrounded with a wall a few inches high, dusted with red holy powder and almost hidden by a flower. Every few feet some symbol appears.

The path twists past the famous mosquelike temple with all-seeing eyes painted on the dome; past dozens of versions of the monkey god; past all-seeing eyes everywhere—painted on a stone, carved on a wall over a door, or symbolized by two mirrors on a temple door; past the brightly painted, hideous image of Kali, with her necklace of heads and a body crushed beneath her feet, her mouth grinning in a mask of evil and destruction, of which she is the goddess.

Every few yards the symbols, the gods, the temples, the carvings grow more elaborate, more detailed, more articulate, up to the last and the largest temples on the zigzag way—the temple with the monkey-god gate, open only to those of the sacred sect, and the pagoda temple carved with the postures of love in uninhibited variation.

Everywhere, the all-seeing eye

. . . like every other farmer's house

The morning often hides its coming in a mist that is cleared by a brilliant sun rising above the snow tops of the Himalayas. On crystal-clear days it reveals Mount Everest's peak.

In the early mist the mountain paths and crude roads are dotted with Nepalese farmers coming from the hills and along the valley with their treasures of vegetables for the markets of Kathmandu.

The wind is ceaseless and the dust endless on the roads. And in the fields the farmer works, breaking up the tough soil with a handleless plow that bends his body to the ground with each spade turned. His head is wrapped in a gray cloth against the dust. His eyes look out with patience, kindness, and fearlessness on his small fields, terraced up the hillside, and his square brick house, painted—as is every other farmhouse in the valley—the orange clay color from the ground to above the door and, from there up, yellow or white.

Along the road the farmer, dressed in his white peg-top pants and tunic, black vest and cummerbund, and headcloth, balances his baskets of vegetables on a pole across his back. In the Kathmandu market by the monkey-god gate he will set up his baskets along the stalls, among the most lush vegetables in the world: shocking-pink radishes over a foot long, Balenciaga-green lettuce as big as rhubarb leaves, and the green fringe of scallions dripping to the cobblestones from the tiny stalls. A shrine nearby is filled with huge cauliflowers, and a tailor sews on his 1876 Singer on the temple steps. In this country, eighty per cent Hindu, religion is a part of the natives' everyday life, and there is no feeling of intrusion when fruits and vegetables from farms and fields are spread on the steps and in the doorways of the temples. Holy cows wander placidly among the buyers and the sellers.

Cauliflower in the temple

A pyramid of salt glistens on a square of cloth on the cobblestones. The precious white crystals have been brought down from the mountains of Tibet, and the rich salt dealer swaggers about in his black cape and boots. His wife is like a figure from a stained-glass window in her deep-green wool, priestlike robe with pink braid; and long black hair and raspberry-pink cheeks in a swarthy face that glows like a child's.

Wandering about the streets in groups in their heavy dark clothes, the Tibetans stand out among the white-clothed Nepalese like clumps of pine trees in the mountain snow.

In front of the brass stalls they choose the biggest brass bowls to take back with their salt money to Tibet, where brass bowls and trays are a mark of wealth in Tibetan homes that have little of anything in them.

The farmer does his business with the money changer, who sits on a platform with his little mountain of silver coins on a white cloth, and then passes from the square into a courtyard to take his place in a row of other men in front of the temple to have his hair cut. The barber sits on the stone street with his simple equipment beside him. After approving of himself in a small piece of mirror, the farmer passes through the street past many fabric stalls and finally selects a neat little geometric print in blue and brown and greens. Along with it he purchases six yards of coarse white batiste for his wife, who will encase the print between the folded batiste and quilt the three pieces together. In winter it would be stuffed with cotton and quilted. The print is masked with the white batiste or net to give the shawl a delicate look, for the Nepalese wear no bright colors, no gaudy prints. The farmer buys spices and seed and chooses a new hat for himself, also of a print masked with white, a neatly tailored, uneven, slanting pillbox, which he dents on the long side.

As he starts home with his bundles his eyes are filled with pride and happiness.

The sun is high, poking into little streets and under arches.

No bright colors . . . no gaudy prints

A little mountain of coins

The monkey-god gate

At the Hotel Royal life is stirring; bearers move back and forth across the courtyard with morning tea (heavy bread and jam), and along the balcony with trays from the dining room. At the end of the balcony, where the last pillar joins a wing, the sun lays a finger of light across a small green door.

Tonight, next month, or the next, when the summer dusk comes late, next fall when the cold night comes early, the shadows will come and go through the green door of Kathmandu. The names will be different, the people the same: other rajas to lay on a tiger hunt; other Americans to complain; other correspondents to get the news. Who knows what day the biggest door-closer of them all may shut the door to all Nepal and prop a Russian gun against it? There'll be another Polish count to fall in love on sight, and another broken-hearted prince to follow love away from the Valley of Kathmandu.

The blonde will one day—soon, they say—flick the ashes from her black cigar and disappear from Kathmandu, and the sad, burly Russian will race his car up and down the mountainside at night and return at daybreak, always hoping to find her there.

But there will be replacements just as surely as there are at "21" every afternoon at five, or in the bar of the Grande Bretagne every evening at nine.

Erotica under the pagoda roofs

. . . *warmer outside than in*

India

DOORS ALONG THE GANGES

THE NIGHT is cool. A pungent, stinging smoke hangs over Calcutta, rising in stringy gray spirals from the open dung-and-charcoal fires. The blue smoke, restless and prying, creeps under the squinting eyelids of the shawled figures swarming among the stalls and shacks along the road that pushes its way into Calcutta.

The hot, hungry day is over and night is coming, with its struggle to keep warm. Thousands of poor wrapped in rags, are gathered around scraps of fire. The smoke picks up the smell of cooking food and carries it along the road where

kerosene lanterns and torches are veiled in the iridescent smoke. Squatting figures warm their rice over the coals as the crowd surges back and forth across the road and the jam of cars and buses is slowed to a jerky crawl.

Men gather around the bright red, green, and yellow stained-glass swinging doors of the barber shops that mark off almost every block of the long gray street. All over Calcutta at night gray bundles dot the sidewalks and the street fires burn far into the night.

The restless music of the flute repeats its whine like the soft harangue of a hushed family quarrel. The lamps behind the red and green doors go out. Many black eyes are open under the ragged shawls.

At the other end of Chowringhee Road, along the open park, smart restaurants, exclusive clubs, and cinemas cluster around the Oberoi Grand. Firpo's restaurant advertises itself "for the man of refinement," and Prince's is "the restaurant for the fashionable man." Both are both. A miniature outdoor Madison Square Garden flashes spectaculars on *Holiday on Ice,* and a sea of men in white sarongs and long, Western-style shirts pours out of the ice show into the night. Smartly dressed people are flocking into the Scheherazade, a huge inside garden in the Oberoi Grand where pillars of royal palms are lost against the sky and the scent of jasmine and eucalyptus mixes with the bouquet of rum drinks served in bamboo mugs.

The sun rises hot and early in Calcutta. Shops and stalls are opening, and people pass in and out of the Buddhist and Hindu temples. A cow is feeding her calf on the sidewalk and a small herd of goats forages through the streets for food. Sleepy children are holding other sleepy children. People are washing their clothes and rice bowls at the running water that gushes from openings in the stone pavement. A baker sits cross-legged, and a shopkeeper reads a newspaper that opens up as wide as his shop. A crow lights on the back of a cow and is in no hurry to move on.

Around bright doors in the night

. . . like a white plaster box

A small boy in rags tosses a rag ball to another child, using one hand while he holds an infant brother on his back. Many children have others on their backs—there's always someone to care for in India from the time a child can walk; how else could the poor survive?

The sun brightens as the tailor's shop opens like a white plaster hatbox, with palm trees shading the roof. On the nails along the walls are many of the smock-like Indian shirts finished and waiting for the customers. The tailor treadles rapidly with his bare feet. There must be thousands of tailors in Calcutta. Only the rich can buy ready-made clothes.

For the very poor, beauty is no secret: men and small boys sit under a tree or in the shade of a doorway with red squares of cloth tucked in at their necks while a traveling barber cuts their hair, his meager equipment in a small box or spread on a cloth beside him.

There is no violence in all the poverty: there is so little to divide, no excess to fight over. And India is a gentle country.

Nearby, three women sit in the open doorway of a sidewalk temple before a coppery-gold image. Indian boys and pretty girls in white cotton saris, carrying books, laugh and talk in College Street. Old men have started their checker pool on a board in the shade of the buildings.

In the noonday heat, India sleeps: on the hot pavement; in doorways; on temple steps; ricksha drivers in their rick-shas.

A small drowsy girl lies on the counter of a hardware stall (of which Calcutta has hundreds) in a shady arcade among big fluted metal wheels stacked into patterns and small ones strung like bracelets. Mindful of her fresh cotton dress, the little girl lies on a newspaper while her brother watches shop.

A fresh cotton dress

DOORWAY TO HEAVEN

A RICKSHA picks its way along the dark street in the holy city of Banaras, among scattered figures squatting in doorways and lying along the small dark buildings. A feeble lamp flickers at a food stall. The wheels of the ricksha crunch on the pebbles and litter as it halts in the darkness at the end of the street; a square of moonlight is framed by the black shadows of buildings and overlapping trees, and there the moon comes into view over a mosque and the street drops suddenly away in a white cliff of steps that disappear far below into the moon-whitened waters of the River Ganges: doorway to heaven for those of the Hindu faith.

Below the square of moonlight lies a strange, moon-white world of still, gray figures engraved on the stone steps of the vast ghat, shapeless under their shawls, marked by the black shadows that lie beside them. The figures facing the holy river sit quietly, dimly scattered over the endless steps and huddled at the water's edge. The only sound is the soft murmuring of the Ganges. Here and there the fleeting movement of a figure breaks the sculptured, inanimate night.

The distant bank of the Ganges is lost in the white mist and the river merges with the sky; there is no horizon. The night stretches into space. Motionless black eyes look beyond the moon, searching for union with their gods. Each Hindu has his own god—Shiva or Shankara, Rama or Krishna, Saraswati or Lakshmi—any of a hundred gods, all representing the one true god through whom the Hindu seeks always purity, self-control, renunciation, and nonviolence.

A figure here and there slips in and out of the water, dark skin glistening in the light; then, wrapped in a shawl, merges again with the bright night. White muslin billows around a dark figure standing in front of the moon.

Soft Indian voices exchange hushed words as a boat pulls out over the water from the platform where the waves rise and fall, pulsing against the steps, showering a fine spray over the watchers, who strive to get ever nearer the holy river.

A glistening bamboo pole pushes the boat away from the steps of the ghat. The muffled sound of the careful oars begins

द्राक्षासव
मृत संजीवनी
अहिल्या बाई घाट

an irregular "swoosh" as the small boat twists and turns among the black boats bobbing along the steps. The sound of the oars begins to cut through the shiny water regularly and the space of wet moonlight widens between the ghat and the boat, until the small black boat turns with the flow of the river past the minarets, mosques, and palaces that rise along the white cliff of steps.

At the top of the wall of steps the holy city of Banaras faces the moon, with black holes between the balconied palaces where dark streets lead back into the shadowy city. Like an enormous Roman arena, the continuous steps of the ghats follow the river. Many of the ghostly palaces, pink and yellow by day and plastered with signs, are empty except on festivals and holy days when the rich maharajas come to Banaras. But the ghats beside them are used by all to reach the sacred Ganges, once called the Golden River of India and believed to be the second abode of Lord Shiva, flowing down from the original home of Shiva in the Himalayas. Its waters cure during life and give salvation after death, and the ghats are known to the Hindu world as the Main Gate to Heaven.

The boat moves silently and effortlessly on with the current to Panch Ganga Ghat, one of the most sacred of all ghats, where the four sacred rivers of India, the Dhutapapa, Kirna, Yamuna, and Saraswati flowing underground, become one with the Ganges.

The great river flows through the moonlight like a caress, but when the monsoons come it rises gently up the steps four or five stories to touch the palaces and mosques, without violence or anger, but like a great cat stretching from a cramped sleep.

The boat moves nearer the fires of the burning ghat, "Manikarnika," where smoke rises in slow columns along the steps; where a never-ending procession of men in white carry their dead on litters to the water's edge to be sanctified in the holy Ganges. Then a newly lighted fire flares in the night, billowing with incense-laden smoke.

The soul's leaving the old body for a new home is not a time of grief for the Hindu. The fires light the faces of the men (only men attend the funerals) looking down from the steps into the blazing biers.

. always closer to the Holy River

Vishwanath Lane, overhung with cheap saris and cloth, makes a colorful tunnel that snakes through the city's bazaars of brass, scented leaves, jewelry, ivory, religious red powder, and Shiva lingams. Narrow and crowded with cows, dogs, vendors, and people on their way to the most famous and most sacred of all temples in India, the Golden Temple of Vishwanath, the cobblestone passage climbs upward and a stall of flower leis perfumes the way to the golden temple where the sacred image of the Shiva lingam presides.

The temple is truly a golden temple, so laden is it with gold on its domes and turrets and gold offerings at the feet of its images. At the sacred entrance is a sign saying no Christian may enter.

Water runs from the open doorway of the Golden Temple in the narrow, rough stone street, and a holy cow, tawny and bony, stands across the sill of the temple. Hindus in their white muslin dhotis and head shawls push through the doorway with their offerings. The cow finally decides to pass into the temple, where the stone floor is an inch deep in holy water and men and women kneel before the images. The temple is a golden glow of candlelight and reflections of gold. Men and women carry children on their shoulders and bring pitchers of water from the sacred Ganges, sweetmeats, and flowers. The crowds scatter rice festively before the images.

The golden dome of the small temple can be seen only from a distance, looking over the mass of buildings from which it rises. In the cinder temple yard, crowded upon by overhanging buildings and the encroaching bazaar, is the huge image of the Royal Bull, surrounded by pilgrims with black robes covering their faces and enormous silver bracelets on their ankles, stroking the great black image.

Under an umbrella beside the Well of Knowledge a holy man sits on the gravel, his body covered with ashes, his hair matted and tangled, stringing from under a red turban, his clothes only a loincloth draped across his emaciated body, but his black eyes are alive with magnetic light.

Though India is mostly Hindu, Buddhism still flourishes. Sarnath, the sacred shrine where Buddha preached his first sermon when he became enlightened and made his decision to pass on to the world this enlightenment, is just at the edge of Banaras, making it a sacred city for the Buddhists as well as for the Hindus.

In Banaras (originally called Varanasi, meaning filled with heavenly light), India's religious Mecca, money and material things have less value than anywhere else in the world; here a few well to do live, few people work—and those only to exist—and Hindus from every corner of the world pilgrimage to the sacred city of salvation.

Overhung with saris, a tunnel through the bazaars

The golden temple

PARTRIDGE IN THE SUGAR CANE

THE SUGAR CANE grew high as a man's head along the dusty roads: dark green and tasseling; sweet and ripe. Bushy squares of dal and millet broke up the dry Indian plains.

It was just after noon and the heat was thick as the little jeeps hustled along, kicking up clouds of dust that the tireless wind scattered over the yellow flowers and weeds along the roadside. Not far out of Delhi the flat land became more wooded. The road dwindled down to two dusty tracks along a canal bordered with dust-grayed trees. The tracks suddenly turned off across wooded meadows of an estate, and soon the little jeeps found a lane along a mango grove and panted to a stop in a guava orchard.

On the heat-faded grass a large quilted blue pad was spread, and bright pillows tossed on it. The little jeeps also emptied out into the shade a small stove, ice pails, vacuum bottles, guns, baskets, and people. There were Pamela, a chic Indian girl in tapered pants and gold earrings (no Indian woman is ever without jewelry); Humphrey, an American novelist and game hunter; the raja's young cousins from Cambridge; a lovely, gray-eyed young child; a grandmother as at home in slacks as Dietrich; a European with a monocle and four guns, prepared for anything that stalked or flew; and two Indian friends of the raja with whom the raja, a talented raconteur, could keep an amusing story going indefinitely.

Soon cold, bitter Indian beer was frothing in tall glasses. Tiny flat pancakes were heaped with diced chicken, hot chili sauce, and mango pickles, and wrapped into neat little rolls.

Insects hummed and birds chattered in the woods. Small greenish-gold monkeys played in the tall grass and brilliant, Balenciaga-green parrots swooped among the branches overhead, where an owl was causing furor.

The picnic lunch was spread out like a painting: long, green cucumber slices; a tray of small new baked potatoes, with their transparent beige jackets drawn tight; mango pickles; rosy radishes; celery; and a diminishing stack of the tiny round pancakes. A growing pyramid of green peas, to be eaten raw, were shelled into a bowl; these, it was declared, were always eaten raw by Americans—I never had, but I did.

Plump cold partridges from last week's shoot were lovingly sliced onto a pale green lettuce leaf (the size of a platter) by the raja himself. Thick slices of rough black bread were spread with mild yellow cheese from America (there is no cheese in India).

Bearers appeared from nowhere with huge brass jars of cool water, and the shadows passed over the bright pillows and stretched off through the tall grass.

It was nearing the hour just before sundown when the partridges, having fed all day on the sweet cane, rise up to the trees for the night, calling to their mates.

Beyond the meadows in the lingering light, fields of sugar cane, tall and dark, stretched in all directions. Slowly the sunlit tips of the cane disappeared across the fields like candles snuffed out, and that strange, still hour—not night, not day—dropped over the meadow and the orchard. It was quiet everywhere.

Then the sound of the cooing whistle rose from the dark fields of cane: one here; again one on the other side; another—another—— The men picked up their guns and walked across the meadow and then the birds started to leave the cane fields. One shot was followed by another and another. The men walked on into the fields.

Tea, cakes, black bread, cheese, and guavas from the trees were ready when they came back in the dusk with the fat partridges.

Along the country roads the night was turning blue; it was the hour when the cows returning home raise the dust into a mist. The white adobe villages were gray in the dusk. The tree-darkened roads were filled with sacred wild peacocks rising in flight to roost in the trees when the car crept among them. The last fading light picked up their iridescent splendor.

By ten o'clock we were back in Delhi at the Oberoi Imperial. A sultry Italian band tugged at you every minute to dance. Diaphanous gold-glinted saris floated over the dance floor with men in dinner jackets. Pamela was lovely

in a pale yellow, gold-embroidered sari, and the handsome Madam Paranjoti was in black chiffon.

Indians are great raconteurs, and we settled down to hunts long past and shoots yet to be laid on . . . the tigers bagged . . . the tigers lost.

Instead of having open season for game, as in America, anyone can shoot at any time, but lots are drawn for blocks (areas in the jungle). It's a matter of luck who gets the most sporting block. Each shoot can take a given number of tigers from the block in a two-week period.

Last year there was the posh shoot laid on by a maharaja for three gentlemen from the West. It was a superb block and there were two hundred beaters to beat the bush, fourteen elephants saddled with silks and cushions; bearers by the dozens; two aide de camps for each guest; two orderlies for each aide de camp. A ten-piece brass band, uniformed in red, played hit tunes from "My Fair Lady" and "The Bells Are Ringing" before breakfast. A staff of superb chefs served dinner and French champagne every evening. With all of this show, the beaters (it is surmised) routed out tigers like clay pigeons, tigers that were so old they had long ago turned in their social security cards, and even non-union tigers. Young tigers were, no doubt, brought out to see the sights, and panthers longed for stripes to take part in the fun. The beaters beat, the band played, the tigers flashed their stripes, the guns roared—not a tiger was bagged! Finally the party resorted to the kitchen shoot for sport. (The kitchen shoot is allowed every party for food during the hunt.)

Another member of the dinner party recounted a hunt at the same time in an adjacent block: just a small party bagged four tigers (the allotment) with four elephants, a dozen beaters, not even a record player or a flute to charm the tigers.

As the evening stood still, there were fighting tigers, ferocious tigers brought back to life, hunts in the forests of Assam, and partridge shoots on the rich estates of maharajas for four hundred guests.

Long after the "cornets in cream" (browned spun-sugar nests with three cream-pudding-filled cones in the center) and the black India coffee, the stories went on. Madam

Paranjoti had traveled all over India by car, train, plane, river boat. We moved from tigers to temples—the temple of Khajuraho with over eight hundred life-size sculptured figures covering the walls in tender embraces of love, built by the Chandella Kings in 1001, dedicated to Lord Shiva. And the Caves of Ellora and the even more ancient Caves of Ajanta, chiseled from solid rock by pious Buddhist monks of the second century B.C., the wats, chapels, and monasteries of the caves completely covered with paintings and adorned with sculpture depicting the life of Buddha and the history of that age.

We were the last to leave the dining room; even the music had gone.

In the kitchen doorway of Delhi's most famous restaurant hang chickens ready to spice, rub with sour-milk curds, bake, cover with delicious Indian sauce, and serve: the famous chicken tandouri for which the Moti Mahal is so world-renowned. The dozens of chefs and helpers in the tiny kitchen overflow into the alleyway.

A dozen chefs in the kitchen

Their famous food has brought the King of Nepal, the maharajas of Jaipur and Indore, United States Vice President Nixon, and ambassadors from all countries to Moti Mahal's marble-topped tables, jammed together in the tiny restaurant where flowers blossom in huge brass bowls and a neon jukebox blasts out Indian music.

Two of the five proprietors (brothers) have flowing handlebar mustaches and never change expression, whether describing a sauce, greeting a guest, or ringing the cash register. Like all good Indian cooking, the food is delicately spiced or curried.

New Delhi was built up around Old Delhi and Old Delhi is built around a big mosque sacred to the Moslem minority. Stalls and shops formed a circle around it.

At the northern gate of the mosque enclosure the Ivory Palace reveals its treasures: the brass room; the silver room; the diamond room; the gallery of antique carved sandalwood and the modern-day miracle of patience, a full-size, carved-ivory drawing-room set that took two men twenty-five years to complete. It's worth its weight in pearls, they say, but worth more than that to the Ivory Palace, where it brings thousands of sightseers, including Prime Minister Nehru; the William Randolph Hearsts of New York; Lady Mountbatten; President Sukarno of Indonesia; the King of Nepal; Lady Oakes; the Robert McCormicks of Chicago; Senator William Knowland; the Douglas Dillons of Washington, D.C.; the Prince and Princess of Luxembourg; and hundreds more. So the guest book reads.

The guest book reads much the same in the unique Emporium of Ganeshi Lall in Agra, really a museum of jade, rare jewels, antiques, and tapestries, among paintings and sculpture. The "Star of Taj," the 100-carat star ruby, glows here along with "The Pride of India," a tapestry (inspired by the rug of the famous Peacock Throne) with eighteen thousand gems set on blue and ivory velvet. Starting in the center with a huge garnet embedded with a diamond, the pattern spreads over the gold-fringed rug into three hundred and sixty-five gold and silver flowers, each different and bejeweled with thousands of forty different kinds of gems.

In the ruins of Kutb outside Delhi, the capital of the Pathan kings, stands the Iron Pillar attributed to the fifth century A.D., miraculously untouched by rust or corrosion. This ancient Hindu relic is surrounded by a gallery of exquisitely shaped and engraved stone pillars on one side and on the others by crumbling walls, arches, and gardens. Nearby are the tombs of the pagan kings, articulately inscribed and unmolested.

Capital of the Pathan kings

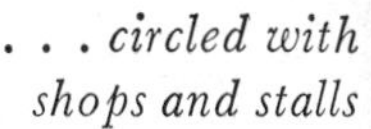

. . . circled with shops and stalls

Along the flat road from Agra to Fatehpur Sikri brazen little monkeys by the hundreds play in the grass and trees that line the flat road. Though they eat their weight in crops, they are sacred in India and run free and wild over the plains.

Mongolian gypsies camp in the dusty weeds and sand along the road, stopping passersby with dancing bears and performing dogs. They collect old hats, canes, anything that passes them off as entertainers, and move about the vast country carrying their beds that always set up on legs, goats, dozens of children, and huge pottery jugs for water.

Long-horned white oxen jog noisily along past the gypsies, pulling a wagon covered with an embroidered, fringed red cover. Inside is a bride. From the covered wagon, above the clinking harness and rattling wheels, drifts a wailing sound, for the bride is required by custom to wail in sorrow as she leaves her home, all the way to the wedding. The wagon is stopped by the gypsies and the curious bride peeps through the fringed curtain, wailing loudly and tearlessly as she does so. Ahead of the marriage wagon is a smaller wagon of musicians; behind is a cart loaded with the bride's clothes and a piece of furniture: her dowry. Other carts and wagons follow and men walk beside the procession. Many of the country wedding party's white dhotis and shirts are spotted with colored water, which is thrown as if it were confetti at wedding celebrations and on other festive occasions that end with a colorful, though wet, effect.

On the road to Agra

Dancing bears, old hats, and dozens of children

Inside —a wailing bride

An entrance worthy of Akbar's palaces

Through the decaying arches of the deserted city of Fatehpur Sikri, the plains of India spread out in fields of millet, wheat, barley, yellow mustard, and dal; orchards of gray fig trees, dusty-green olive groves, and tall grass.

An enemy approaching Fatehpur Sikri about 1575 A.D. would have been forced to make his way across a lake at the foot of the city in the face of its defenders, scale its massive fifty-foot walls on the other three sides of the six-mile enclosure or fight his way through one of the seven gates guarded by brave and strong men of the Grand Mogul Akbar, greatest Mohammedan emperor.

Green pastures now stretch across the plains where the blue lake once reflected the red sandstone parapets. The massive walls lie torn and crumbling.

Its great Buland Gate is the tallest gate in all India (176 feet). Its wooden doors, studded with iron horseshoes and framed with an exquisite arch of tile, mosaic, and carved stone, made an entrance worthy of the great mosque, acres of palaces, tombs, art, and treasures.

Now the doors are open and the sun at will sends a shaft into Akbar's rosy palace city, guarded only by a barefoot, turbaned keeper.

Fatehpur Sikri, the Emperor's beautiful dream palace, was abandoned in fewer years than it took thousands of men to cut the rosy stone from the hills and shape them into endless galleries, palaces, pavilions, and acres of paved courtyards. For centuries the hollow city has towered majestically on a

The crumbling arches of abandoned Fatehpur Sikri

hill above the plains of India near Agra, its terraced roofs taking their grace from the Buddhist viharas and minarets, its arched galleries poised on thousands of carved pillars defying the ravages of time.

The deserted city unfolds: the blue mosaic roofs of the Turkish Sultana's palace of pink stone and delicate mosaics; a palace for Emperor Akbar's Hindu wife; houses for his harem of 5000 women; gardens; a hospital; baths; the hall of audiences for Akbar, a temple of four religions for his wives; a pavilion for entertaining; a palace for the powerful and loyal prime minister; a three-room house, called the "hide-and-seek house," with stairs in the walls onto the roof, where the Emperor played hide and seek with the ladies of the harem (a very popular game with them).

In the center of the largest courtyard, about two blocks long, is inlaid a life-size parcheesi board in black-and-white marble. On a platform in the center of the board the royal players sat and pondered their moves, which were carried out by beautiful dancing girls who moved from square to square, performing the plays in a graceful dance. It would seem this might have made it hard for the players to keep their minds on parcheesi, but this is the way Akbar, and often his favorite wife or his guests, whiled away an hour.

There was also a house where men representing all religions—Christian, Moslem, Buddhist, Brahman, Shiitic, Parsic, Jaina, and Sunnites came every seven days to Fatehpur Sikri for religious discussions with Akbar.

The red sandstone piled up into more and more structures. Great stables stretched out with stalls for one hundred and ten horses, and fifty camels, with rings cut in the stone for tethering the thoroughbreds.

The first palace built at Fatehpur Sikri was for Akbar's Hindu wife (the second of his four wives), because of whom Fatehpur Sikri came to be.

The city was deserted, it is said, because of a shortage of water, but perhaps Akbar grew tired of Fatehpur Sikri after sixteen years, or lost his belief in its power to bring him good fortune, as it did on the day he came upon the village of Sikri (near Agra, then the capital) as he returned from a campaign in the central plains of India. Here Akbar begged the Mohammedan saint, Salim Chisti, who was known for his miracles, for the son and heir he had been denied. The saint bade him bring his Hindu wife, Mariam-Uz-Zamani, to reside in Sikri. He did so, and within a year a son was born. So delighted was the emperor that he made Sikri the capital. For twenty years, day after day, the city grew.

Grateful to Salim Chisti, Akbar erected for him a tomb of solid white marble in the center of the court facing the Gate of Victory. Poetically carved and fretted (considered one of the most beautiful examples of ancient carving in India), a white pearl in the rose sandstone city, the saint's tomb lies below a cenotaph of solid mother-of-pearl inlay. Through the marble filigree beside the cenotaph hundreds of threads of colored yarns are tied. The legend of the tomb of Saint Chisti says that any wish made when the string is attached to the fretted marble in the saint's tomb will be granted—as was Akbar's—a sort of spiritual string around Saint Chisti's finger (there's a small fee attached to all of this). Although the wish of Akbar for an heir was granted, the dream of the magic of Fatehpur Sikri vanished in some sad way.

But the red city stands through the centuries, empty and echoing the bark of wild prairie dogs and the chattering of monkeys through its hollow halls at night, and haunted with the soft laughter of the ladies of the harem in their baths or gardens, and the tinkle of bells on the ankles of the dancing girls with their veils drifting in the night breeze; peopled with shadows of beautifully gowned women, richly robed men, and distinguished visitors of the court once so private that he who entered it unbidden was put to death.

As centuries passed, Akbar's kingdom was looted by invaders and other kings, scattering the treasury of jewels. The great Koh-i-noor diamond, along with the Peacock Throne of Shah Jehan, was carried away by Persian conquerors.

Almost within sight of Fatehpur Sikri, Akbar lies in his five-terraced Buddhist vihara mausoleum at Sikandra in the garden of Bahishtabad, where in the recess of a pedestal over his tomb the Koh-i-noor diamond once lay, its white brilliance glowing in an eternal fire.

DOORWAY ON THE JAMUNA RIVER

As man has striven down through time to immortalize himself or another in stone, Shah Jehan, in memory of his young wife, Mumtaz Mahal, created the Taj Mahal in a garden on the banks of the Jamuna River at Agra. To enfold the one so profoundly loved, Taj Mahal was molded, sculptured, and hewn from pure white marble by twenty thousand men working over ten years, each surely empowered by some extraordinary inspiration. Preserved records of payment for services of artists, inlayers, engravers, colorists, mosaicists, designers, dome and turret makers, from thirty-seven countries, come to a staggering amount of rupees. The records show the purchase of more than forty different kinds of jewels, semiprecious stones, marble, pearls, onyx, shells, stone, coral, chrysolite—imported from all parts of the world, taken from the sea and the land.

The workmen were well paid, their wages equaling annually the entire income from at least thirty villages.

As the white marble rose in the garden and cast its shadow across the water, 'Shah Jehan's imagination turned the shadow into his own black marble tomb, to stand opposite the Taj across the quiet river. But the black shadow had scarcely been crossed with the first blocks of black marble when the Shah, in his last, unhappy years, was imprisoned by his tyrannical son, Emperor Aurangzeb, through whose guilty conscience he at last came to lie, instead of in his own black tomb, beside Mumtaz Mahal in the pale Taj.

Through a door within the bronze doors of the main gate, the Taj Mahal is delicately outlined: a wordless poem composed in the heart of one man and translated by thousands of other men into stone. With its moonlit dome and minarets reflected in the cypress-bordered water of the marble canal, it is no more possible to describe than it is to *see* the fragrance of the rose in its garden, to *hold* in one's hand the moonlight that traces the poetic dome, to *taste* the breeze sighing in the cypress, or to *inhale* the song of the night bird.

Thailand

THE GOLDEN DOORS OF BANGKOK

COLOR and smell associations, as they stay in the developing fluid of the subconscious, seem to grow clearer, and on the slightest added stimulus give back vivid impressions, developing details of images that were at one time seemingly out of focus. Just as a perfume can chain a woman to a love affair forever and vice versa, so at the word "Seville" I can smell oranges and roses, the sweet heavy fragrance magnified a thousand times by the hot Andalusian sun. From a small garden of roses surrounded by orange trees, a hundred images of Andalusia unwind in my mind.

The other way 'round, I can scarcely smell the smoke of a lighted match without having thrust in front of my eyes a picture of the dung fires along the road to Calcutta on a chilly spring night.

Practically all countries are a color impression. To me, Japan is red-and-blue neon; Egypt golden alabaster in the desert sun; Seville the smell and color of oranges; Madrid shocking pink, the color of the matador's cloak; Cambodia, the gray and green of the forest and the temples of Angkor.

A streak of moonlight falls across my terrace, and the whole Kathmandu Valley pours over me. Bangkok is printed on my subconscious in gold—pure, unalloyed gold. Every time I pass Tiffany's, Bangkok dazzles my eyes:
Gold Buddhas standing, lying, sitting in rows of hundreds;
Gold doorways to wats, bôts, and pagodas;
Gold Garudas, the divine vultures with the heads of men;
Gold elephants looking down from the Temple of Dawn;
Gold-traced porcelain inlaid in walls;
Gold Nagas, serpents that live underground and bring rain;
Gold bracelets and jewels shimmering on the Royal Dancers;
Gold stupas;
Gold spires on a hundred temples;
Gold barges with golden oars for the king's oarsmen;
Gold Kinnara, a gentleman with the body of a bird;
Gold Kinnari, a bird-lady with a rose in her hand;
Gold altars containing someone's bones;
Gold leaf fluttering on a thousand images;
Gold candlesticks by the millions in gold viharas (chapels);
Gold shawls for the emerald Buddha in winter;
Gold costume for the emerald Buddha in the rainy season;
Gold raiment for the emerald Buddha in summer;
Gold hats (three) for each of the Buddha's costumes;
Gold-leaf print curtains at the Royal Theatre;
Gold teeth, both upper and lower, though the wearers would prefer black—gold teeth proudly flashed by young and old;
Oceans of gilt and glint and make-believe gold;
Golden mosaics by the square mile;
Golden tile up, down, and around; on top of, and under;
More golden than gold, the saffron robes of the monks.

Gold Buddhas sitting in rows

Gold stupas

Fluttering gold

Gold-traced porcelain

Gold Kinnari

Gold armor

The Royal Compound, which is actually a walled town of temples and palaces, is like a golden sun around which not only Bangkok but all of Thailand seems to revolve. The satellite temples all over Thailand pale beside it. Within this one square mile there is probably more oriental splendor than in any other square mile in the world.

Other, lesser lights in this tiny country: the teakwood forests; jungles of wild tiger, deer, boar, bear, and elephant to hunt; forests alive with exotic birds, parrots, peacocks, and myna birds.

There are plains and mountains, waterfalls and lakes; seaside resorts on the Gulf of Siam and the South China Sea to swim in; the river Menam Chao Phya twisting across the country, through the heart of Bangkok, like the coiling serpent (naga) that adorns the temples.

The most famous door in this glittering, golden maze is the entrance to Wat Phra Keo—Temple of the Emerald Buddha—door of teakwood inlaid with mother-of-pearl in the most intricate design of mythical animals encircled in rosettes, framed with a pagoda of teak carved into delicate black lace encrusted with mother-of-pearl. The entire temple is gold and blue mosaic with a bordered base of Garudas holding a daisy chain of golden serpents, completed with a blue tile roof and golden spires.

I keep evading the indescribable Emerald Buddha with pencil and paper, (cameras not allowed) but here we are before the exquisitely carved, green translucent image in raiment of gold and precious stone. The sacred image looks down from a high altar so ornate that it becomes a confusion of gold, precious stones, and crystal, with statues rising on tiers to the feet of the exalted Buddha. This mysterious idol, known as the Emerald Buddha, is really carved of one piece of green jasper stone, sixty centimeters (about two feet) high, and sits under a golden canopy. The image has three changes of vestments—for the rainy season, the winter season, and the summer season—with three headdresses of pure gold set with precious stones for each costume. The ceremonial changing of the raiments is done by the king. For many centuries the so-called Emerald Buddha, which was cut in India, passed from one temple to another in the states

The Emerald Buddha—three changes of costume

or kingdom of Siam, but was finally brought by the first king of the present dynasty to the Wat Phra Keo in 1468. Every inch of the interior walls around the translucent image are covered with murals of the many lives of Buddha.

Buddha, like Christ, forbade his followers to worship or create images after him, but the Buddhists, as did those of the Roman Catholic faith, created images supposedly to remind them of their one God. They do not worship the images of Buddha any more than Catholics worship statues of Our Lady of Perpetual Help, the Virgin Mary, or the saints.

Ninety per cent of the Thais are Buddhists, including my friend and her daughter, who were both educated in a Catholic convent. Other Buddhists told me there were three cardinal rules by which the Buddhists live: Reject sin; Do good to others; Keep a clean heart. A man of Catholic faith two months earlier in Rome had given me rules by which he lived: Renounce sin; Do unto others as you would have others do unto you; Keep a pure heart.

Through the arched doorway of Wat Po is glimpsed the head of the great reclining Buddha. Over 160 feet long and more than thirty-nine feet high, this colossus represents Buddha entering nirvana, 543 B.C. Gilded from the beautiful face to the pearl-inlaid feet, the body is a gentle expression of serenity and peace.

In every other arch of the long gallery is a small reproduction of the reclining figure, fluttering with millions of gold-leaf squares that form a quivering halo around it in the reflection of the flickering candles. Thin blue smoke rises from the incense smoldering on the little altars. Saffron-robed monks sitting along the white arches, the huge gold figure, the sweet smell of the incense, the candlelight, all create an extraordinary mood.

Reclining Buddha—
one hundred and fifty foot colossus

Entering Nirvana, 543 B.C.

The fluttering tips of the gossamer squares of gold leaf, pressed with a fleeting gesture to the images when incense is lighted in prayer, pulsate in the faint breeze, seeming to give life to the figures. Over many years, millions of the shimmering offerings have distorted the shapes of the statues where the gold piles up over the heart, the forehead, or over the eyes. Some parts of the images are scarcely gilded.

In the temple yard, almost every tree is different—a casuarina tree, a magnolia heavy with huge blossoms, a blossoming fruit tree, and clipped spinde. The heat magnifies their heavy fragrance.

Door carved by a king

In another wat in the palace precinct, the most sacred image of Buddha is seated above his eighty disciples on the sacred altar wherein rest some of the bones of the Great King Rama I. A gallery following the enclosing wall is lined with hundreds of sitting Buddhas with flowers, rice, or water in offerings at their feet; a scrap of red silk in the hand of one, or a saffron ribbon across the shoulder of another.

To King Rama II is attributed the exquisitely carved teak door to the Vihara of Wat Sudhas, the chapel of Heaven of Indra. Deer, boar, bear, birds, flowers, monkeys, all mingle in a verdant jungle scene, imaginatively carved out of the heart of the black teak that gives the scene mysterious depth beyond the skillful carving that was the devoted and painstaking work of years. Hundreds of architects, artists, and woodcarvers decorated other doors from slabs of teak for the temple. It can be understood that an ancient king should perform some humble and creative task on a temple of Buddha in a country where today the young King of Thailand, Defender of the Faith, has worn the humble saffron robes and carried the little yellow bag during the time of his priesthood.

Almost every man, during his youth, enters training for the priesthood. He may or may not become a monk, for his vows are not eternal, but the training prepares him spiritually for his lifetime. Many men, therefore, in their youth have had shaven heads and worn the saffron cotton cloth, which is a phenomenon of color, cast in two shades that are never seen anywhere else: a yellow so intense it can be seen at a distance beyond ordinary perception although a multitude of other colors surround it; an orange-saffron that fuses the color of blood oranges, clay, and gold, discernible long after the absence of the sun has negated every other color. The length of the cloth is wrapped so that it leaves one shoulder bare.

The young priest begs for his food, which is deposited in his jar, and gifts, which he carries in a yellow satin bag often embroidered "Give to the poor." These gifts set the board for the monks, other young priests, and the poor. Also standard equipment for the saffron monk is a large black umbrella which protects his shaven head and bared shoulder from some of the hottest heat on earth, streaming down from the sky in devastating continuity and turning the stones of the streets of Bangkok into grills. These young monks walk the streets barefoot on their missions. In the temple courtyards they sit on the grass in groups looking like a huge crepe-paper flower with its petals unfolded. The young priests stand in a semicircle, silent, smiling, and enjoying the fun while a youngster in the temple yard exercises his salesmanship to market his parchment rubbings from the temple walls. They graciously pose for a photograph, but they say nothing.

Late at night, along a remote country road, the saffron robes will appear before the headlights of a car. On the sweltering streets by day the young priests move along under the black umbrellas, always—always—smoking cigarettes and often wearing dark glasses.

The Thailand Buddhists, though they go to the temples on special religious days, have altars in their homes where they perform their religious ceremonies each day.

The high walls enclosing the temples and wats are pierced with many gates guarded by lions and Garudas. At others are huge stone Chinese monsters, which the Thais sometimes mischievously refer to as "ballast"—their way of expressing their lack of admiration for the Chinese figures (so unlike Thai art) and inferring that they were brought from China merely as ballast in the ships' holds.

Standing sentry at the wall doorway of Wat Ratbopit are simple soldiers carved in deep relief on wooden doors. Behind this wall are rows of serene, gilded Buddhas, and bôts filled with treasures, precious stones, gold, and works of art.

Saffron monks and Chinese monsters

In contrast to the gold, glitter, bronze and stone inside, the wooden soldiers are very touching and gently amusing in their eternal vigilance. Their weather-grayed uniforms change slightly from door to door, indicating a different branch of service on guard. With the paint faded from their uniforms, their guns held at attention, the wooden soldiers swing aside to admit almost everyone, leaving the half-monsters and lions at the inner doors to make the final decisions. But the brave soldiers can be very strong: when they stand side by side and the iron bolt is shot across their backs, no one can pass.

Brave wooden soldiers swing aside

The purest example of modern Thai religious architecture is Wat Benchamabopit, of Carrara marble with triple pagoda roofs. Here is where the present king served his priesthood. Facing the marble courtyard at the back of the temple, framed in a golden doorway, is a beautiful black Buddha.

The hands of the thousands of Buddha images are in many positions, signifying many things. The image often seen in Thailand is with one hand raised to "hold back the waters of the river," but it takes two hands to "stop quarreling among relatives." In many images Buddha is using two hands, trying for 2500 years to stop family quarrels, but they still go on. However there is less disagreement among Buddhist families than those in Western countries, I'm sure.

The King served his priesthood

Patterns of metal in a doorway to me stand for Bangkok as a city—big, not beautiful, noisy, mechanized. Like the many metal shops, it is orderly, forming a pleasing design of its many ugly utilitarian parts. A city of trams, buses, markets, narrow streets, there are, on the outskirts of this city that loves sports and entertainment, lovely homes, clubs, and a race track.

The boxing matches, which begin late in the afternoon, rank next to bullfights in color, excitement, and danger. The dusky-skinned boxers wear exotic colors of shocking pink, magenta, purple, and pale blue, and fight with their feet. It's a kick to the left ear, a knee to the right jaw—and anything goes. Prayers to Buddha are said in the ring before

Ugly, utilitarian . . .

Behind the last dancer—gold-encrusted curtains

starting, in an exquisite posture on one knee with one toe pointing upward, like the naga moldings. The accompanying music is barbaric and rises to tremendous excitement and frenzy at times of climax in the bout; other times it keeps up a stirring wail that would incite murder in the breast of the most gentle.

A great black Garuda stands decorative watch at the gold

and black doors of the museum, modern in design, yet traditional. The white, austere building fronted with green-lollypop spinde trees is another example of modern Thai architectural design.

In the quiet theater, gold-encrusted, purplish-black curtains close behind the last dancer in the long, glittering finale that passed across the lower stage, through the curtains to the small backstage rooms: a golden barge carrying exiled princes, a mourning queen, and a forgiving king, followed by a great entourage of child dancers (many start training for Royal Ballet at nine) in the most elaborate costumes of silk, gilded and ornamented with jewels, with golden-spired headdresses, their ankles and arms stacked with bracelets.

The orchestra platform is empty too. The gooseneck light still burns where the chorus of five sat around a small table, watching the script, chanting, supplying voices for the masked dancers who were interpreting the most intricate situations and delicate emotions with their movements and eloquent hands. Back of the voices, the musicians had sat, supplementing, leading, embellishing the story the dancers were enacting with strange music from oboe-like instruments, woodwinds, xylophones, drums, cymbals, and gong. They too have vanished—the play is over.

The khon, or masked play, is so beautifully enacted, the story so romantic, the plot so childlike, the costumes so dazzling, that it becomes an exquisite grown-up fairy tale come to life. A story of royal twins and the queen mother, wrongly accused of infidelity, exiled in the forest (one twin was born of the queen, one supplied by the seer for companionship). The king comes upon the young princes, attempts to destroy them unknowingly; they battle with arrows that turn to sweets and flower petals that rain down on the stage (which always happens when relatives unjustly quarrel). In the final scene, after much beautiful dancing, chanting, and music, the once-exiled and still-unforgiving queen calls on the gods to hide her from the king, who has forgiven all and seeks a reconciliation. Mother Earth obliges her by opening up so that the queen literally drops down through the floor of the stage, which opened up to save her.

The elaborate drama told in dance takes place on a

rectangular stage that, through lighting effects and curtains, becomes two stages where a short scene or flashback can be played on the second-story stage. A third stage that is just one step above the audience is a platform that runs in front of the real stage and extends past it, with exits at both ends.

With gods doing miracles, tying villains up with curses, magic rings to keep things moving, and seers producing half of a pair of twins, there is nothing cumbersome or static about the play.

The Thai plays and dance are thrillingly beautiful entertainment but, strangely enough, the Silpakorn Theater itself, which is the national theater school, lacks splendor.

The doorways and the life of the poor in Bangkok are mirrored in the Menam Chao Phya. The houses stand in the water on stilts, their porches overhanging the banks of the river where the dwellers bathe, wash their clothes, and fill their jugs of water.

At dawn the floating market fills the river. A boat brimming with a vegetable garden drifts past the doors along the banks. The river looks like an hors d'oeuvres platter of fish, prawns, small red peppers, bowls of pimiento and rice, small onions, and seaweed, as the boats anchor among the stilts for customers to make their purchases. A boat of oranges, bananas, papayas, tangerines, mangoes, rose apples, and melons

Black Garudas stand watch

floats like a fruit bowl down the river. Flower-garden boats are heaped with orchids, gardenias, hibiscus, petunias, and roses that color the water with their magenta, lavender, pink, and purple reflections.

Sampans glide among the market boats, filled with coal, or wood, and poultry to be sold to markets in the main part of the city. Women gondoliers do the stiff-legged ballet of the gondolier—one step forward, two steps back, in their sarong skirts, coolie coats, and cone hats.

I did not see one Siamese cat.

The river—a platter of hors d'oeuvres

Cambodia

THE DOORWAY LOCKED BY THE FOREST OF ANGKOR VAT

THE BRIGHT SUN dappled the dirt road as it entered the forest of Angkor. As the forest thickened, the fan-shaped trunks of the banyan trees spread into walls as wide as the road and the sun no longer penetrated the dense foliage.

The road ahead was swallowed up by shadows. It stopped suddenly before a doorway choked by the massive roots of the banyan trees that tore through the stone, sprawled over the walls, and twisted around its crumbling tower: a door locked by the forest, doorway to the lost temple of Ta Som at the edge of the forest of Angkor, imprisoned by the tropical jungle when the ancient cities on the Cambodian plains were deserted.

The lichen-mottled stone and roots were one grotesque struggle that had endured for five hundred years. The jungle vines and trees had won, but they were now imprisoned by the stone, victims as well as victors. All through the vast tropical jungle the vines and trees and lianas clawed the great stone temples and monasteries apart, cracked open their vaulted domes, and crushed the beautiful images in the chapels. Roots forced their way into the cracks and wove their tentacles into doorways and galleries, pulling down the engraved façades with their weight.

The trees of the forest looked old and gray, as if wearied with the struggle. But other young banyan trees eagerly spread their viperous roots to absorb the proud, crumbling temples. These gray-scarred trees are the beasts of the forest, devouring all things around them, stretching their huge, boring, twisting roots for hundreds of feet above the ground.

Scattered leaves drifted along the flat, sandy ground around the darkened, locked doorway of Ta Som. The road turned knowingly away among trees taller and less tangled, where the sun leaked through the leaves and turned the vaulted ceiling of the forest into a mosaic of yellow and green, with tiny pieces of sunlight and bits of shadow.

Finally the road widened and was crossed by another. A patch of sky broke up the mosaic, and suddenly the forest ahead was filled with black doorways, peering like hollow eyes through the shadowy leaves. The gray- and white-li-

A phantom in the jungle

chened towers of Bayon Temple in the lost city of Angkor Thom took shape in the jungle like a phantom. The monstrous pile of stone stretched for blocks, its maze of towers rising higher and higher in the center like a fountain. The ancient, bud-shaped towers revealed huge faces of the Bodhisattva Avalokiteçvara, faces on domes as tall as three men, which, thousands of years ago, had put the Khmer world under the benevolent protection of Buddha. The eyes were closed in meditation, the benign features broken, chipped, and torn away by the overgrowth of hundreds of years. The ornate headpieces and chignons had broken away, but the countenances were stronger than the forest and as peaceful as the pale blue sky that came through the clearing.

Broken, mold-stained steps ascended perpendicularly to the second and third terraces, where the beautiful bud-domes rested on tiny chapels, sanctuaries, and monasteries, with some of the Buddha faces near enough for me to reach up and touch the lips. The walls of the temple, once engraved with stories of war and victories and carved with the history of the ancient Khmers who built and deserted Angkor Thom, had been defaced by despoilers and the forest. Fragments of carvings of Apsarases (celestial dancers), birds, flowers, animals, remain around the hollow doorways.

Through the dark doorway of a small vihara vaulted and domed with the four faces of Buddha, a linga stone lay broken but adorned with a silk ribbon, a wilted flower, and an offering of water in a flowered cup.

Hundreds of hollow, black doors gaped along the galleries and looked out from the ruined porticos. Distant doors ended the rows of topless pillars and stood at the top of endless stairways leading nowhere. At the end of a terrace a flight of steps dropped down into the heart of the temple, ending before a hollow doorway through which a mysterious trail moved on from one shadowy chapel to another, from one beckoning doorway to the next. A faint scent of incense mingled with the acid, moldy smells. Here, deep in the heart of the Bayon temple, a trickle of smoke arose through a doorway and spread out on the flat, heavy air, rising from a tiny chapel where a broken image was outlined in the dim light,

Under the protection of Buddha

propped up by flat stones. The smoke hung around it like a veil rising from the smoldering incense sticks stuck between the broken feet of the image, over which a few grains of white rice were scattered.

The feeling that someone had just passed through each dim doorway was insistent. Always there was the echo of a soft leather sandal on the rough stone, a glimpse of a saffron robe passing through doorways that receded one inside the other to a mere black spot. The call of strange birds and the wind in the forest accented the loneliness of the lost city.

Angkor Thom, more than once the proud city of warriors, kings, and beautiful women, temples, palaces, harems, courts, shops, and towers, was ravaged by conquerors and, finally, the jungle. Abandoned hundreds of years ago, the site was too vulnerable to attack, too accessible by river and across the plains.

Even before the temples of Angkor were abandoned to the forest, other invaders had many times burned and pillaged them, destroying the gods and defacing the temples. Angkor's cities were last rebuilt after the Cham fleet had attacked by way of the Mekong River about 1177. Three times started, not finished, deserted, rebuilt, captured and

Through a hollow doorway, the benign features

forsaken, the fourth and last Angkor was finally abandoned in 1432. Abandoned, as Khmer history prefers? Or was its whole population obliterated by some strange catastrophe?

And then men came again with axes and elephants and pulled the jungle vines and trees from the walls, hacked the twisted roots from the images and altars that were shapeless masses of leaves and moss, an incomprehensible labyrinth of mystery and danger.

The different periods of architecture and religious relics remain mixed in the ruins of the six hundred brick and sandstone temples, tombs, palaces, monuments, and sanctuaries in the forest of Angkor, in sixty square miles of stone-wall enclosures and dry moats which have lain on the Cambodian plains for centuries. Many lakes and canals were once filled with water from sources now unknown.

From Bayon a road led off into the forest, promising to tell more of its secrets, reveal more of the mysteries of the lost cities, and uncover more beauty. But it only contradicted and confused and withheld, the farther it was followed: past the bas-relief elephant wall suggesting the outlines of the great sprawling palace, to courts and servants' quarters; around the banks of the great dry lakes that promised the secrets of their lost sources; through the Victory Gate supported on the backs of three-headed elephants nibbling lotus

The gods were helpless

The forest —victor and victim

blossoms, watched over by the four-faced towers repeating the same half-told stories; and the hundred sea gods and sea devils that guard the bridge over the river at the gate told no more.

Even images of Lord Shiva and the stone gods guarding the doors of the temples were helpless at the hands of the forest; their staffs were broken from their hands and the invincible gods were tied with vines and rendered helpless. Even Naga, the serpent feared by all men and all things, had battled with the banyans. The huge twisting tree roots had grappled with the stone serpent, and in the death struggle had pulled the great serpent from its balustrade and held it, broken, to the ground for centuries.

Deep in the ruins a banyan tree clung to a crumbling chapel altar, almost in an attitude of relenting, with its long, craggy roots holding the stones almost as if in an embrace.

Thousands of artistic hands had followed the Khmer architects, carving light embroideries of figures, stones, Apsaras, images of Vishnu, Shiva, elephants and the lotus blossoms, Naga, and gods riding on the divine vulture, Garuda. Some-

Angkor Vat—a white mountain

times the statues of four steeds stood waiting near a holy image so that the god could speed away at will.

Between Angkor Thom and Angkor Vat the forest thinned to a light woods, where the passing river had kept the forest back from the great pile of stone, and the temple of Angkor Vat stretched like an undulating white mountain along two square lakes. It would have taken days to climb all its stairs, visit all of its chapels. The Palace of Versailles or Vatican City would be lost in its structure. It was miles from its gopura (gate lodge) to the highest tower of the monasteries where the saffron monks still live in the sanctuary of the enclosed and private gardens.

Royal palms measured their puny height beside the towering bud-domes engraved with the four faces. A thousand hollow doors looked out from the terraced galleries.

The late sun sent horizontal rays through the doorways, and here and there touched a pillar or an archway to mark it in the deep shadow. The halls went on and on, the stairs up and up, under pagoda roofs that rose higher and higher to the peak of the sprawling temple, which, because it was originally a funeral temple, faces west.

At the end of a high, open-sided gallery running between two vast courtyards like a bridge, a small vaulted chapel was stacked with idols. A dozen images of Buddha stood one in

Many things had been said

back of and above another. Before the images was a low altar, like a stone bench, where incense burned and candles flickered. The sun was reaching through a hollow window, falling in a shaft across the altar and touching a huge brass bell with a brilliant streak in the dark, shadowy alcove. There wasn't a sound from the vast halls below, or the corridor, or the stairs. After a while I had a sensation of being watched as intently as I was watching the smoke rising from the altar. The strange quiet and the statues in the shadowing chapel were very unreal and absorbing. I felt someone near and sensed a movement in the shadow by the prayer bell. I turned my eyes from the altar, and a priest stretched out his hand shyly with a stick of incense held lightly in it. The hand turned slightly in the direction of the brass bowl that had dozens of smoldering sticks of incense stuck in the sand and ashes, making fine threads of smoke that rose slowly and billowed out in a fragrant haze before the dim altar of images like a screen.

I took the incense and lighted it at the candle, and another gray thread rose from the brass bowl. After a few moments I bowed to the priest, who stood in the darkness by the bell, his black eyes shining luminously from the shadows. He put out his hand again, and this time there was in it a small mallet, which he offered me. I took it and approached the bell, which now had one small patch of sun drawing a target on its big brass surface. The priest raised his hand toward the bell and I touched the target with the mallet. The muffled note rolled from the big bell and the dark hand indicated the bell again, and then a third time. Then the hand closed and dropped away into the shadow, and there were a dozen bells rolling through the gallery, multiplied in the halls below. They were ringing in the dark stairway. The temple was filled with the three notes like the prayer that goes on and on. I listened: the three notes were rolling over the temple, fading away. The brown hand accepted the shiny, worn mallet. There had been no words spoken. In a fleeting second I saw a look of pleasure in the quiet, dark eyes. I turned away with the feeling that a long time had passed since I came upon the altar and that many things had been said.

At the top of the dark stairs, I thought I could still hear the bells down the corridor ahead of me as I descended the last long hall and emerged into the late daylight. Along the terrace that looked out on the lakes, a huge standing golden Buddha in a vihara was draped with strips of red and yellow silk. The fragrance of flowers and incense mingled around the gilded figure, and a barefoot priest in white jacket and black dhoti was placing an offering of two red flowers stuck in large flat slices of sugar cane . . . an offering of sweet food, fragrance, and beauty.

Inside the narrow portico the pillars threw shadows deep into the opposite walls; the beautiful bas-relief of three Apsarases was outlined in the fantastic headdresses of the

Before hollow doors—bas-relief

celestial dancers, and the hollow black doors of Angkor Vat stretched back along the portico as they have for centuries.

The sun was down, and the too-short tropical dusk was cooling the forest and quieting the birds. It was time to leave the forest, but the dusk seemed lingering on, and there stood in the dim light the gopura (gateway) of Ta Prohm, the enormous monastery that had not been rescued from the jungle. At the lodge gate my car left me and drove out of sight around the five-mile enclosure to meet me at the opposite gate. For the light—even I knew—would not last to retrace my steps back through the forest. The forest was a dull gray; I was alone before the doorway.

A beggar in black rags stood inside the shadows just beyond the gopura. I passed him and started down the sandy, narrow path that too quickly disappeared into a fallen doorway, the beggar following behind me like a self-appointed bearer. I tried to discourage his following me, but he spoke only Cambodian and only looked at me and smiled, stopped when I stopped, moved on when I moved on.

Ta Prohm has been left as it was when the buried cities of the tropical jungles of Angkor were discovered after hundreds of years of abandonment. Only a narrow vague trail from gate to gate has been cut through the center of the enclosure. The rest of the walled monastery enclosure of temples and terraces and viharas is locked in the impenetrable forest.

By the time I had traveled along the path through a string of dark chapels filled with fallen stones and broken idols, I realized that my driver's protests had been well-founded. The chapels were black, the beggar was black, and the path wound through a maze of passageways, over fallen walls, among topless pillars and doorways overgrown with trees and vines that were connected to fragments of buildings disappearing in the tangle, sealed by the forest and piles of stone. The banyan trees formed walls larger than the fragments of the buildings—some of them twenty feet across their spreading, viperous roots, zigzagging and overlapping like an encampment of towering gypsy tents, their grayish-beige bark discernible in the fading light. The roots wound like snakes

Viperous roots, like towering tents

over each other, over walls, and piled up in big mounds, lying across the path to be stepped over. They obliterated the path and their formation made new passageways. Finally I felt my way out of a long, dark enclosure by touching on stones and broken sculpture piled in the narrow corridor. I came out into an overgrown courtyard with many hollow doors, scarcely discernible, leading from it, and I realized that night had overtaken me. There were fallen arches dimly outlined and there was no indication in the darkness of the vague path. I turned and looked behind me to the man in rags. The shadowy figure stood almost imperceptible by the doorway I had just left. I stepped aside . . . there was a pause. As he stepped lightly in front of me, I saw on his lips a gentle smile. His eyes were cast down and he proudly offered me the end of the gnarled wood staff he carried. This way we walked on through the jungle, in and out of small chapels, along crumbling terraces and roofless corridors, over stones and roots.

The trees were full of the black shapes and strange subdued calls of birds. The beggar stopped suddenly as big wings left the wall above and whirred past. Stone tumbled from the wall along which we had been feeling our way and fell among the roots and tangled grass. More stones followed into the tiny opening at the end of the wall. We retraced our steps and climbed through a crumbled arch of the wall that was filled halfway to the top with huge stones. On the other side of the wall a large, sandy courtyard was outlined on one side with door frames and on the other two sides with the jungle. A stone figure stood before a door leading out of the square and a stone lion guarded another doorway. In the dim light they looked real, and I almost wished they were.

*In the darkness—
tangled roots,
black doors*

Finally the stick guided me up several steps, and I heard my heels on the sandstone blocks of a terrace. From the center of the terrace a dark tunnel of trees ended in a distant circle of light, and I realized this was the path from the temple to the gate at the opposite side of Ta Prohm.

We paused for a moment and I looked back at the last black door of the forest of Angkor. At the end of the path I said good-by to the beggar as he stood quietly, his white teeth showing in a smile as he melted into the forest. The beggar was richer, and so was I.

It was the night before Chinese New Year and the fires were burning all over Asia, as they were along the road from Angkor Vat to Phnom Penh. The scorching day was coming to a close and tomorrow, in the little Buddhist country of Cambodia, was the most festive day of the year. In every village, on each remote farm, it would be a day of religious celebration, a sort of wiping the slate clean. All debts must be paid; all useless things disposed of; old family quarrels mended or forgotten—a time to start a new life and clear the land for new crops. Across the flat plains the harvested fields were set afire as the day ended and men left the fields. The blaze stretched out along the roads, here, hundreds of miles from Phnom Penh and with Siem Reap far behind.

Saffron-robed monks with black umbrellas folded under their arms walked along the remote road in twos, their brilliant robes visible far in the distance.

Bonfires burned all along the little clumps of houses, and people ate rice and pink melons by kerosene lanterns.

As it grew dark, all across the plains red streaks lighted the sky and silhouetted the palm trees like a sunset. The smoke from the burning fields smelled sweet. As the night passed, the plains turned to low hills along the great Tonlé Sap River winding across Cambodia, merging above Phnom Penh with the Mekong and Siem Reap and flowing on to the sea.

In a few hours the dusty road would stop at its bank, where a small ferry would link the little road with the other shore. There it would hurry on to Phnom Penh, the charming little capital city of Cambodia, its broad, tree-shaded main street balancing on the banks of the Tonlé Sap.

Hotel Le Royal is set back from a shady avenue in Phnom Penh, in its own little park with gravel drive and flowers.

I turned off the whirring fan that hung like an airplane propeller from the ceiling of my room. The noise was much like that of a rushing locomotive, but the fan did keep the huge room, which had an eighteen-foot high ceiling, cool. Though it was like sleeping in the path of a tornado, it blew the mosquitoes away. The large alternating ginger and white stone squares of the floor were cool, and a small balcony overlooked the dining garden, bordered with banana trees and strung with lights, to which I was about to descend.

I closed the door and did as I had been requested by the bearer—hung the key on a hook six inches from the keyhole. Why, I did not know, but I followed the system.

The stairway, banistered in dark, polished wood, rose the five tall flights from one end of the lobby and zigzagged up, touching four dimly lighted corridors with floors about the width of Madison Avenue, of black and white stone squares.

Halfway down the long, shadowy, windowless top corridor there was a banistered circular well that, I observed, opened through all of the five floors down to the lobby. As I turned away from the banister of the well, I stopped cold and froze—down the wide corridor padded a tiger. With its head dropped and its shoulders moving up and down, it undulated down the middle of the hall. I noted without much comfort that it was not full-grown; neither was it a baby. It flashed through my mind that Cambodia is famous for its great forest of tigers and elephants, but I was hardly prepared to find one in Le Royal. The tiger's big paws made a muffled sort of thud on the stone. Now I could see its wide amber eyes, and it had seen me. I felt like stone. I thought (in a sort of paralyzed way) that the tiger might mistake me for a statue. I was too shocked to figure out that he could hardly have eaten his way through the hotel up to the top floor—or, if he had, he couldn't be very hungry now unless he'd saved the top floor for dessert. I wasn't thinking—at least not thoughts.

The beautiful beast was not wandering or faltering; he was padding along as if he were on his way to an appointment. I sort of madly hoped it wasn't an impromptu dinner engagement.

At a distance of about ten feet from me he stopped and lifted his big, beautiful head above his shoulders and looked directly at me. I couldn't have looked away because my eyeballs were stuck.

In this long moment (the greater part of my entire four-months-long trip), I heard the racing of feet up the wooden stairs far at the end of the long hall and a high, excited voice calling, "Oola! Oola!" It wasn't for me, I was sure, so it must be the striped one being paged. The tiger turned his head to look behind him, and a breathless woman with a chain in her hand half ran and half flew down the corridor, followed by two wide-eyed bearers.

The tiger turned his attention back to me and lifted a paw, crossed it over toward me, and set it down to change his course in my direction. As the chain clicked around Oola's neck, I exhaled for the first time in ten minutes. The lady was apologetic about turning me to stone, and I only managed to break my face up into a sickly grin . . . "Oh, it's nothing at all . . . nothing at all."

After Oola had been tugged away, staring back at me over his shoulder with big yellow eyes, I managed, with the aid of the banister, to steady my shaking knees enough to reach the ground floor, where I stopped off at the lovely little bar in the corner on my way to the garden. There I ate a "picky" dinner, during the course of which I learned it was a matter of wager around Le Royal as to whether or not the lady would give Oola to the zoo at the psychological moment or have the bad judgment to wait one day too long to find Oola had grown up. Whenever leaving my room thereafter, I stepped outside, called my bearer from his cubicle, and had him beat the bushes before I ventured down the corridor.

In the streets of Phnom Penh saffron-robed monks with black or white umbrellas moved quietly along, carrying their bowls and their saffron bags, begging for food and giving of the spirit.

The Royal Palace enclosure is a glittering world of pagodas, red lacquer, and gilt Naga moldings, surrounded by a high yellow stone wall. There is a pagoda where the young royal princes and princesses start their training in the Royal Cambodian Ballet at the age of seven. There are lovely drives and a swimming pool; the Palace of the King; the Hall of Thrones, which is all yellow velvet, gilt, red lacquer, and crimson, where I was received by the King of Cambodia; and the palace of Prince Sihanouk, where I was received by the Prince, but the Gentleman from Cambodia is another story.

There are lovely homes, sailing clubs, sports clubs, night clubs, and movies in Phnom Penh.

In the center of the town is a market of canvas-covered stalls; a street of the famous Cambodian silver; and rows of shops selling gold necklaces and earrings. The streets of the town are broad and busy, filled with bicycles and bicycle-cabs, cars and motor bikes. The buildings and walls are often touched with bougainvillaea or pale lavender flowering vines. There's a boys' school in grass-roofed pagoda dormitories and an impressive women's college.

The impressiveness of Cambodia is in the spirit of its people, who are serious, gentle, intelligent, and happy. Whatever the future may bring to Cambodia, at this writing it is eager to mind its own business; to be sincerely a neutral country; to improve itself; and to live peacefully among its neighbors. No foreign ideology is allowed to be fed to the people and the people do not seek it out. The government is interested in keeping the Khmer traditions and a friendly independence. In all Asia I saw no more progressive, happy country, its people untouched by the strife, hates, and tensions of the world.

Giving of the spirit

serious, intelligent . . . happy

Viet Nam

LUCIEN'S DOORWAYS

I HADN'T seen Lucien for almost two years until we met again at the Grande Bretagne in Athens, where every foreign correspondent in the world, including Lucien, was poised, ready for flight toward the Middle East to get a last peek through the closing doors of the East—or to take off to Paris on the slightest pretext for a tidbit on royalty, riots, or Russian remarks. Lucien looked much the same, though his love of good food had triumphed. But he was tall, still very handsome, and spoke, as always, in a gravelly, hurried voice.

Lucien was on his way to Saigon for the longest of all assignments: "indefinitely." He knew Viet Nam well and insisted that he would show me Saigon when I reached there.

Two postcards en route declared that he was awaiting my arrival, and he *was* waiting at the airport almost two months later, on the hottest day in the world, with a lemon squash in each hand, when I stepped off a plane into the melting heat.

I didn't realize this meeting with Lucien was to prove a rare event and that it was never to happen again during my stay in Saigon.

It was only a few minutes' drive across the flat, open country until we were in the broad streets of Saigon, vaulted with the spreading branches of stately trees. Lovely, summer-resort-type houses were set close together, with gateways that opened onto gravel drives—a French city of parks, squares, vistas, and the sidewalk cafés that the French take with them wherever they go.

We drove three times around the city market and down

the plaza filled with cut flowers and potted plants brought down from Dalat. Lovely Saigon women were filling their arms with flowers and gliding away in bicycle rickshas, on their own bicycles, or on motor bikes, with their long tunics of silk (ao dai) floating in the breeze.

Along Tu Do Street smart shops that were once filled with chic French clothes and jewels now display native or American merchandise. The fading of the tricolor left Saigon drifting between the casual American dollar influence and the reform government of Ngo Dinh Diem's family, which was bleaching the local color out of the lovely city, known once as the Paris of the Orient.

Leafy Tu Do Street ended at the banks of the broad Saigon River, where the old Majestic Hotel sat only the width of Ben Bach Dang from its tree-lined banks. We arrived at about five o'clock, and the big wicker chairs of the Majestic's small sidewalk café were filled.

Lucien took me to the reception desk and said he'd pick me up at seven.

My room was big but cozy, with just enough of a balcony to open the doors and look out over the slow, sparkling river and down the broad street that followed its gentle curves faithfully across the city. It was a beautiful, balmy evening—like Bermuda on a July night.

It was quickly seven o'clock, and a French voice from the reception desk announced that Mr. Bradenhurst, "a friend of Lucien's," was in the lobby. A small boy indifferently maneuvered the two-passenger lift slowly down the three floors, and I stepped off into the lobby, where an extremely thin, very British-looking man identified himself (with an accent that confirmed his looks) as Peter Bradenhurst, and explained that Lucien had been detained and it was his pleasure to take me to the dinner party to which Lucien had failed to tell me he was taking me.

Peter knew everyone at the large buffet dinner that ended at little tables in a garden lighted by dozens of flaming torches. It was here that I met Madame Ngai, the most "alive" woman I've ever known and certainly one of the great women of Indochina. Not as tall and willowy as many of the beautiful Vietnamese women, she was vivacious and bronze, had flashing black eyes, and wore a pink print ao dai, with gold loop earrings and a great gold necklace. She talked with everyone and was very gay and stood out in the large international crowd. She said Lucien had told her he was bringing me to see her three hundred children tomorrow. I had heard already of the famous An Lac home for children. The story of Madame Ngai had been told to me—of the children she had picked up, wandering and lost, each day of the war when she went into the villages at the end of bombardments to gather them up, terrified, hurt, and lost. At the fall of Viet Nam above the 38th parallel, many babies were thrown across "the line" to save them from becoming prisoners, and young protesting children were pushed across to freedom. Some parents were shot fleeing, and the children wandered away. From all over, children of the war, mixtures of all nations, were gathered together by this woman. Children still continued to flow into An Lac, and Madame Ngai brings them up as if each were her own.

The next day Lucien called me to apologize for not having picked me up the night before, and said he was again detained but a friend of his was coming to take me to tea with Madame Ngai. A short while later a young woman called me from the desk and said she was "a friend of Lucien." She was a beautiful Vietnamese girl in a print silk ao dai, high-heeled clogs, and long black hair done in a chignon.

We were met at the gate of An Lac by at least twenty-five small children, all neatly dressed, clean, and polite. Many of them bowed or put out their hands. There were round, opaque eyes, black eyes lifted at the corners, blue eyes, pale skins, and bronze skins.

We had tea with cinnamon, from lacquer cups in Mme. Ngai's parlor where little girls sat on the polished floor, cutting and sewing little coats and dresses from a pile of pale blue blankets. There were familiar insignia on the blue blankets and the words "Pan American World Airways" printed on each, for these, I learned, were faded blankets no longer usable on the lush Pan Am clippers and were sent to help Madame Ngai clothe her children.

A priest came and gathered together many of the fair children from the gravel play areas and little houses that made up An Lac, while the little black-eyed Buddhists were marched off to the nearby temple.

Before I returned to my hotel the Vietnamese girl and I shopped for gold necklaces and looked at fabrics in the Indian shops along Tu Do.

Lucien later called me to say he had planned a trip up into the country tomorrow. We'd leave at nine o'clock. I thought it couldn't happen again—whatever it was that was happening to Lucien to detain him ever since I'd been in Saigon—so I was ready at nine on the clear, hot morning and was having orange juice in the café when a Volkswagen stopped along the street and a man's head appeared over the boxed hedge that enclosed the café: a nice, clean-cut American face with an army haircut. As the slight, blond man approached my table, I noted he was a captain. He was "a friend of Lucien," and was taking me to Thu-Dau-Mot because Lucien was detained. He also had a camera and was agreeable to photographing our way, mile by mile, to Thu-Dau-Mot if I liked. The young captain had been in Saigon for many months and was studying the language because he wanted to know the people he lived among in order to understand them. He felt this was part of his job as an American officer. The captain knew a great deal about the country and drove to some new part of the tiny country each day off and weekends, even as far as Angkor Vat in Cambodia.

An Lac—
happiness,
serenity

At the edge of a sugar-cane field on the road to Thu-Dau-Mot, a Buddhist shrine sheltered offerings of rice in a flowered bowl, a small bottle of water, fresh sugar cane, shreds of silks that fluttered in the hot wind, and smoldering incense set before the gods by the farmers of the rich Mekong Delta. The blue and yellow designs painted on the white-washed brick and plaster of the shrine stood out in the white-hot sun. The heads of Naga (the serpent that controls the rains) formed the moldings on the tiny roof. The little shrine with its offerings to Buddha was like many that scatter over Viet Nam in the Tonkin Valley along the Annamese Mountains of Viet Nam, and across the rich Mekong Delta where rubber and tea grow on big plantations.

Shrine in the sugar cane

In a clearing near a clump of six or eight grass-roofed houses the Catholic cross rose out of the fields on a one-room, gray-and-white frame church. Two Vietnamese women in white ao dais and a white-robed nun crossed the heat-blistered road under a black umbrella. As we left the church, the captain spoke politely to the Vietnamese women in their language. They had a twinkle in their eyes and answered back with the same greeting, which sounded quite different, but they were pleased. The captain laughed quietly and said, "Well, at least they knew what I meant."

Although Viet Nam is fundamentally a Buddhist country where a mixture of Buddhism and other oriental religions is practiced, its president, Ngo Dinh Diem, is Catholic.

A Catholic cross in the fields

It was the season of Tet, Chinese New Year, and houses, villages, and shops along the roads were each in some way made festive. A bicycle shop had flags and a huge, multi-colored star that shone in the sun and whirled. It may have said, "Gasoline, 10 cents a gallon," or, "Tires Repaired"—but it was festive. The proud owner of the shop was gentle and obliging and, like any Shell Oil station attendant in his desire to perform a service, struggled to communicate directions by pointing and gesturing. In the little house next door, where he lived, we were offered tea in lieu of water by his beautiful young wife, surrounded by three quiet children. He wore an expensive wrist watch, of which he was very proud. The captain asked him the time and they had a cigarette together.

In Viet Nam the pig may not be kept in the parlor or the barber shop, but here along the road to Thu-Dau-Mot it

. . . like any Shell Oil attendant

A pig in the doorway

lay at the door in the shade of the house, where rows of bottled soft drinks sat on the cool dirt floor. A pedestal at the gate offered food, water, and incense to the garden god or the land spirit.

By legend, a spirit lives in the house or on the land, and when it is occupied a place must be made for the spirit to live, so that he will be happy and the new occupant will be untroubled. Sometimes a wooden or plaster house or temple, as in Thailand, is mounted on the pedestal. Man and woman dolls are placed in the house, also servant dolls and a cow and dog. Food and water is set before them so that they will be happy.

A small girl casually whirled a hula hoop along a remote dirt lane beside a pyramid of *nuoc-mam* jars. The little girl's father was a part-time fisherman, like thousands of other Vietnamese who bring in the great harvest of fish from the sea and the roaring Mekong and Saigon rivers. The captain went to the door to ask the father if we could photograph the little girl.

The crude pottery jars in banana-leaf and straw slings were piled up in many yards, to be refilled with *nuoc-mam*, the fermented fish sauce that is the first and last sign of East Asia from Japan to India. High in protein and vitamins—and flavor—*nuoc-mam* is to this part of the world what garlic is to Italy, curry to India, and salt to the West. It flavors every native dish from soup to pastry; it even returns to flavor the fish itself, and is one of Viet Nam's chief exports.

If there was any doubt as to who had the right-of-way along the roads, it was the Volkswagen of the captain that waited, and we halted in the village of Lai Thieu while beautiful Viet Nam girls in white ao dais waited for a driver to attach a bicycle to the side of a cart. These tall, slim women of Viet Nam are truly the most beautiful women in Asia and move with the grace of dancers, carrying themselves like

On the road to Thu-Dau-Mot—
a hula hoop

Market in slow motion

princesses. They entered the small cart with more grace and poise than most women clamber into a Carey Cadillac. They sat on the floor erect, with their long legs folded under them gracefully.

Thu-Dau-Mot is a busy little town, the streets jammed with people on pedal and motor bicycles, with trucks and carts. The market place at the end of the rectangular cobblestone center is covered wall to wall with merchants squatting on the cobblestones beside baskets of tangerines, vegetables, spices, shoes, leftover boxes of Tet greeting cards, a stand of books, fish, and rice. It was barely possible to squeeze among them, bargain over other heads, and push slowly through the squatting market.

In the middle of the market the captain bought a melon, tangerines, and a book. He felt that since we'd trampled all through the people photographing them we should at least buy something.

A woman with a red-checked towel over her head, wearing the inevitable earrings and gold bracelets, her silk ao dai tucked up around her waist, worked over a basket of flavoring leaves beautifully arranged in a pattern that she could deftly pick up the leaves, count them, and toss the piasters (coins) onto the flat basket in one movement. The market had a tranquil, slow-motion quality, as has all Viet Nam.

In the rectangular plaza opposite the market of Thu-Dau-Mot, buses were leaving with people carrying produce from the market. On top of one bus sat a beautiful young boy with a brilliant pink cloth on his head. His two proud gold teeth, dark skin, and luminous dark eyes made a curiously exotic and lovely picture as he sat on bags of grain surrounded with cans of petrol, empty baskets that had brought vegetables to market, and bundles of tea, spices, and fruit. He spoke a little French, and before he was signaled by the driver to climb aloft we talked—he was eager to be friendly. He had brought

Gold teeth and a pink turban

bags of rice on the top of the bus from his father's farm to the market. As the oldest son of a Vietnamese family he had great responsibility. In most homes worship is carried on at the family's own altar table (there are only a few large temples in Viet Nam) with rituals of candles, incense, and tablets that represent the family's ancestors in the Confucian religion. The oldest son performs these rites.

Finally people and packages were loaded and the small bus lumbered away. The boy stretched out his long, thin arms as the bus bounced down the road out of sight.

The elephant tusk is the sign of the lacquer shops and studios for which Thu-Dau-Mot is famous. Here huge lacquer paintings cover the walls and everything from tables to ash trays are laboriously created in the dimly lighted back rooms of the shops by old men seated on the floors and young men painting with gilt, Chinese reds, and white.

Faded color and traces of gilt covered the walls of a decaying temple slumping agedly in an unkempt garden nearby. An ancient mandarin strolled among the overgrown walks. As we wandered through the wasting garden, the frail old man slowly turned his steps toward us. He asked if we liked the garden and if he could help us to see it. The captain made a great and gentle effort to understand and to speak with the old gentleman as we walked through the garden together. The mandarin spoke gently of the flowers that were blooming in lost confusion, the uncut branches of the trees, the misshapen hedges, as if they were in perfect order. As we left him by the wall of the garden, we bowed and thanked him. He bowed more deeply and said, in a thin voice in Vietnamese, "I am obligated." These graceful words are the basis of Vietnamese life, obligating a man to his father and mother the day he is born for giving him life. Throughout his life he acquires obligations for everything that is done for him. The idle "thank you," mechanically spoken and immediately dismissed, does not exist for the slightest favor or pleasure. Everyone has obligations to his doctor beyond the paying of a stated sum of money. A successful man often receives a modest salary, but has a sum on which he draws to pay his obligations for favors or help he has received through his life.

The obligations to parents are never finished. President Ngo Dinh Diem's biography notes that his four brothers are a politician, a bishop, an ambassador, and—according to Vietnamese tradition—the youngest looks after his mother.

We returned to Saigon in the cool early evening, and the captain had to report for duty at eight P.M. I'd seen the ugly American, the quiet American, and lots of defenseless Americans. The captain was the thoughtful American, of whom we need many more abroad.

To be sure, Lucien called again that evening to check whether the trip was good. I was about to ask what his dilemma was when he said he'd pick me up at nine o'clock to show me Saigon by night. I was ready at nine and began to wonder what "I'm a friend of Lucien's" would bring tonight. At nine-thirty I had begun to consider whether Lucien had possibly run out of friends. But the phone rang. A strange voice from the lobby identified itself as "a friend of Lucien's" . . . The next time this happened, I must refuse this ridiculous situation or find out what was going on, but it *was* pleasant to see Saigon in such a delightful way.

I am obligated

A charming Chinese by the name of Sing stood at the desk. This man was a rare Chinese—a tall one. With that charming reserve of the Chinese, Sing made the same explanation and said Lucien had suggested places we should go, but if I didn't like these places we'd go elsewhere; but he felt I must see Cholon, the old Chinese city overlapping Saigon.

We walked among the bazaars along the narrow streets that were a mass of lanterns, a continuous volley of firecrackers, and festive decorations still celebrating Tet, the New Year season. Cholon is the business part of Saigon, a city of trade and industry where the big rice markets are carried on. We followed Lucien's plan and danced at the Arc-en-Ciel, a huge place, two orchestras and as dark as the Fairy Chimneys at Göreme. We stopped later at the night club Tu Do, where beautiful Vietnamese hostesses looked like fashion models in tight silk Chinese sheaths slit to their stocking tops.

The next day, as Sing was taking me to the airport, I asked him were Lucien was and what had happened—as I had asked Peter, the Vietnamese girl, and the captain, each of whom had replied, "Oh, he's all right. He sends his love and says tell you he'll call you tomorrow,"—and Sing said, "He'll probably be at the airport if he isn't detained."

We arrived just in time to go through customs, say good-by, and for me to find myself on my way across the field to the plane. Sing was waving from the cool, glassed-in café of the terminal, and passengers from a plane that had just landed were making a jagged line across the field from the other direction. And there, suddenly—to my amazement—I saw Lucien. He saw me and ran toward me, waving and talking as he came. Before I could ask what had happened, he said, "Did you have a good time? Didn't I show you Saigon?"

I said, "What do you mean—I never even saw you!"

"I had to leave for Japan late the night you came. So I lined up my friends with a program. Did they stay on schedule?" he asked. "Did you have a good time?"

"Yes, I had a wonderful time! But if you were in Japan, who called me every day?"

"Oh that—" said Lucien, as the stewardess pulled me through the door of the plane, "that was a friend of mine!"

Singapore

By day, the heat and the river and the quiet

DOORWAYS IN THE SINGAPORE NIGHT

THERE is an intensity about Singapore, the tiny mongrel island too small for a world map to contain its printed name, broken off from the tip of Malaya in the South China Sea by the Tebrau Strait.

The heat has actual dimension, something you can reach out and touch; it stacks up in the doorways and corners of buildings during the day. The flowering trees are heavy with perfume and the orchids are velvety and deep.

The Malayans (mostly Chinese) have a tender sobriety and disturbingly quiet eyes. Singapore has a motionless quality; the jungle close by seems to wait; the tall palms move too little; and the sea seems to stand still. Men in lavender or violet and pink sarongs sit in the street shade; women in wide black Chinese pants and coolie coats drift gracefully along the streets under black umbrellas.

Just passing through the lounge of the old Raffles Hotel, along its dimly lighted corridors or courtyards, has implications of drama. The big tropical garden with towering pillars holding up the blue-black sky makes the Hollywood world seem real. After a late dinner with my Singapore hosts in the Raffles' Elizabethan Grill (the most elegant dining in Asia), we drifted into the lounge for coffee. The deep-cushioned bamboo lounges and chairs grouped around little tables on acres of flowered carpet were empty of all but a few travelers (by British Crown Colony Time, twelve o'clock is late).

On the far side of the lounge sat a young man, obviously American, with crew cut, square face, blue eyes. He was not a traveler, possibly a foreign correspondent, I unconsciously observed as we were seated at a table nearby, next to the row of open windows and in reach of the same and only remaining waiter.

Two amber-filled glasses arrived at the man's table as we sat down. Almost immediately a singularly pretty Malayan girl came through the door and directly to that table. Her clothes, though native cotton, had been turned with a determined effort into Western dress. She was slim and tall on her high heels. The man and the girl looked at one another for a long second. The girl's golden-brown face was expressionless, but her quiet eyes had broken up into a thousand words when she looked at the man. They sat together, speaking quietly and occasionally. Her soft English, with an accent, and his slow American English drifted to our table. Long silences were filled with the long, steady look between them.

Every night for weeks, at twelve o'clock, the man had been there . . . then the girl . . . so "they" said.

The following evening I returned to the hotel about one o'clock from Prince's, a dinner and cabaret club on Orchard Road, where the best curry "is" and where the beautiful and rich of Singapore go. Some of my friend Daphne's delightful Chinese clan had taken me, and we stopped in at the Raffles' lounge, as does everyone, for a night cooler.

The young man sat at the table alone. The two tall glasses were waiting. He was attempting to scribble on a piece of paper, but kept scratching out and starting again. I looked at my watch: it was 1:15. He put the pencil away and stuck the paper in his pocket. He stared at the table, holding his glass tightly as if to hold back the minutes. He didn't drink, just held on tightly to the glass. As each person left the lounge, at every movement of the door, he looked up, but finally let go of the glass as if he could hold time still no longer, shoved some coins into the waiter's hand, and hurriedly left.

As we were leaving the lounge at two o'clock, the waiter handed me a folded piece of paper. "You dropped, ma'am."

I said good night to my friends and walked along the long patio toward my room. Under the first bright light I started to stick the paper into my purse, but, seeing it was a cablegram, unfolded it. It was brief:

> OVERDUE IN NEW DELHI TEN DAYS. REPLACED BY L.K. IMPORTANT STORY LOST. RETURN TO STATES IMMEDIATELY WITH EXPLANATION WHILE STILL ACCEPTABLE. PLANE LEAVES SINGAPORE TWO AM FEB SECOND. YOU'RE ON IT.
>
> J.H.R.

 On the fold were the words and phrases scratched out:

"If you'd—— If I—— Why didn't—— You know how much——"

Today was February second; it was two A.M. I automatically turned and started back toward the lounge, to do what I wasn't sure, but I had something personal that had been given to me by mistake. I felt the scrap of paper was not to be thrown away. As I passed the lounge, the girl arrived at the doorway. I saw her face when she looked across the completely deserted room, with the tables cleared as if no one had ever been there.

We passed and, as she turned to leave, I said, "Isn't this yours?" and handed her the paper. She paid no attention; her motionless eyes were looking straight ahead. As she went down the steps, I saw her mechanically unfolding the paper . . . and then she was lost in the Singapore night.

Doorways of small town houses politely set back from the street behind wrought-iron gates and brick-plastered walls that flower with potted plants, with palm trees looking over them from tropical gardens, told of Singapore's past elegance.

Elegant façades with arched, leaded windows detailed in ironwork stand side by side on the old streets. A mosaic of tile lays a carpet up the steps of one house to an inlaid-mother-of-pearl door. Now the houses are peeling and scarred, defaced with signs. Two handsome young Chinese boys emerge in Bermuda shorts and Prince Charles haircuts from one house. At the top of the steps two servants on their

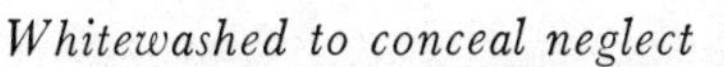
Whitewashed to conceal neglect

Past elegance

A lavender flower in the temple

knees scrub water over the veranda, a courtesy to expected guests, signifying the house has been purified. An elegant old gentleman in long silk Chinese coat stands in the doorway smoking, slightly curious (as curious as a Chinese can be).

The walled doorway to a once-fine house is battered and crumbling, but whitewashed to conceal its neglect, as is the improvised garden wall of corrugated tin. In the yard are several generations of one family, clamoring about a long table set for a midday meal.

Wilting banana trees are bent into an arch over the door of a Hindu temple in celebration of a wedding. Above, a frieze of strangely composed figures intertwined, yet completely disconnected in style, size, or subject, overhangs the roof and builds up over twenty feet into a dome, and scattered along the edge of the sloping roof are life-size images of the holy cow.

Inside the temple door is a stone-floored gallery open on two sides to the courtyard and temples which are not enterable by any except those of the Hindu religion.

A holy man, with tangled, matted hair bound with bands of cloth, wears on his forehead the red insignia of his holiness. Wrapped in his white muslin, his only worldly possession, he shyly gives me his blessings and a small lavender flower from an altar by the prayer bell.

Strangely composed figures

Women drift gracefully along the street

Dusk—a bath from a basin

At dusk, which comes to Singapore in a purple-blue haze, a woman playfully dries a small boy after his bath from a basin and pitcher of water along North Bridge Street, which runs below the bridge at the Singapore river's edge. Along the wharves are bales of cotton; baskets of fish; ropes; crates; litter; and debris. Ramshackle food stalls propped against one another brace themselves precariously on the steps down to the river. The sampans, junks, and big, red-streaked hauling boats loaded with bags of rice, rubber, and pineapple line the river on both sides, and others thread their way home in the fading light of the day. All along this short street, under an arcade, people are washing their clothes, their children and themselves at the end of the hot day. Some live in the junks on the river; some make homes of the warehouses.

The dusk turns a kindly light on the riverbank litter and brings out the quiet, dusty beauty of the people.

From everywhere, people pour into the streets of Singapore as the night overcomes the heat: turbaned Sikhs; Malay women in rich oriental sarongs, kabayas, and loose baju kurongs (Chinese pants); Indian women in gold and silver saris, wearing long gold earrings and jangling bracelets; men in Western shirts, and purple, blue, and lavender sarongs; Westerners, Orientals—rich and poor, young and ancient; people from every part of the world mingling in the cool, welcome dusk. The streets are filled with cars, bicycles, rickshas, and taxis.

In the twilight Singapore stirs like a big, lazy cat that's been sleeping in the sun. Lanterns are lighted in the night bazaars; in the Chinese quarter, shady doorways are filled with shadows that go and come. The street is everybody's home who needs it, and here people crowd with bowls of rice cooking over little fires, sleeping, smoking. Smart clubs scattered along the swarming street of the poor bring big cars, picking their way among the rickshas and people. Gambling and bargaining are a part of the poor's struggle to live and the rich's search for pleasure. Crowds are drifting into the smart restaurants, in and out of the old Raffles, like a movie in slow motion.

The jungle of streets is mysterious, and we are told, "Stranger, walk warily in the Singapore night."

Java

DOORWAY TO THE BLACK SAPPHIRE

JAKARTA, stuck on the tip of Java, trailing along the Java Sea, sweltered in the heat. It was midday and the noisy city had taken refuge behind bamboo shades and under its big shady trees. A few stragglers drifted through the street, and

The old canal—two worlds along its banks

occasional pedicabs, buses, and cars droned by like lazy insects. Dust lay on the leaves of the trees and coated the bumpy streets. One had the impression that unseen tensions and controls lay as heavily over the once-gay city as did the heat.

My taxi bumped over the driveway of the Des Indes Hotel, which squatted half asleep with its bamboo shades drawn against the yellow sun.

In the sticky terrace dining room the waiters were struggling to keep moving from one would-be diner to another with one dish or glass of warm water at a time.

No one at the Des Indes knew or cared if there was a

reservation of three months' standing, least of all the desk clerk. Eventually a shuffling boy lugged the luggage around the side of the old building and up an outside stairway onto a balcony from which three doors opened. One led to a large room, which was mine, with a small screened porch, chintz-covered wicker chairs, and a table. A tea tray soon arrived with baked bananas, tea, and fresh fruit.

The bathroom was a Dutch version of the Early American rain barrel. In one corner a square cement tank waist high was filled with fairly clear water which looked black because of its depth and the dark color of the cement. On top floated a large tin dipper. The tank was too high to scale, so I gathered the idea was to stand beside the tank and pour water over oneself as the natives did at wells in the Java hills. There was a drain in the stone floor of the bathroom, and the commode was raised like a throne on a platform in the opposite corner.

On the balcony an antique telephone stood on a wicker table. This instrument, I found later, was virtually an ornament, since it was pure coincidence if a message ever penetrated the switchboard, seeped through the front office, and broke through to the lounging bearers with enough urgency to motivate one to amble up the stairs to rap on the door and point to the phone. I doubt that it had any connecting wires, which I failed to note at the time. I learned to go downstairs, cross a courtyard, go through a back door into a cubbyhole where a polite old gentleman mastered a switchboard that had enough wires to service the Waldorf, and get the communication directly.

It was soon late afternoon. The temper of the sun had subsided, and it sent a subdued glance down the famous old canal that sliced across the city in front of the hotel. Crowds quickly filled the streets, and I took a pedicab that was still lingering under the shade of a tree and swept with the crowd along the broad canal. The water moved slowly, scarcely disturbing the reflections of the scene along its banks. Men in sarongs gossiped and slipped in and out of the cooling water; women in flowered and striped sarongs soaped their clothes on the stone ledge, dipped them in the water, and did the same with their small children.

Young boys cavorted in the canal and chased naked along the grass banks. And a young girl slipped a tube of cloth over her clothes and wriggled out of her sarong and blouse that dropped around her feet and were tossed into the canal, followed by the girl, wrapped tightly in the cloth. Her black hair floated loose and straight around her lovely face.

Bright sarongs were stretched along the banks, drying on the grass like flower beds under the big trees. Along both narrow grass banks of the canal wide, busy streets were now crowded with cars, little buses, trucks, pedicabs, and quiet-faced, beautiful people pushing their way home through the heat, crowding over the bridges—Indians, Chinese, Polynesians, who had long ago blended like graceful flowers in the garden of Java.

The canal with the native life on its banks and the streets beside it were like strips cut from two different worlds at two distant periods of time and laid incongruously side by side. I walked slowly back through the lovely dusk among the crowd to the hotel to inquire for a message from my friends, the Sastrosatomoses; tried once more, futilely, to locate their address in the phone book. Across the small, dim lobby, I stepped through the doorway of the tiny Sesotya gem shop. Inside, a blond, blue-eyed Dutch woman sat at a small table enclosing gems in small folded squares of paper and placing them in envelopes. A Javanese boy stood beside her. A small cabinet and another straight chair beside the desk filled the closet-size shop.

The woman motioned to the chair and asked me in English if I would sit down. She spoke of the heat and continued to wrap amethysts, topazes, and tigereyes in the little folds of paper; the boy put them into envelopes.

A black star sapphire dropped from a fold and lay in a black translucent oval on my white cotton gloves on the table. The star in the huge drop of black dew gleamed beyond the stone as if it had actually escaped from it. I asked, "How much is the sapphire?" The woman smiled and said, "Do you like it?" and continued, "When did you arrive in Jakarta?" We talked and looked at many stones, but none was as handsome as the one on the glove. I told her I had arrived four days late and I was unable to contact my friends and that they had probably given me up or had been dropping messages into that unconnected phone. She said, "My husband will know them. Have you had dinner?" and added simply, "I am Madam Kusumobroto. Won't you have dinner with us? My husband is picking me up any minute." Almost immediately a charming Indonesian appeared in the doorway, and we got into a tiny foreign car with a driver and drove through the almost-dark streets past the palace, along a tree-crowded park, through widening streets, lined with lovely old houses, and turned into a driveway.

Inside the house two charming young children were introduced and quickly said good night, and we had cocktails at a round table covered to the floor with red-and-black tapestry in a room that had an almost oriental feeling.

Madam Kusumobroto's husband tried to reach the Sastrosatomoses, but with no luck; he could not even locate their address.

Telephoning in Jakarta is about like the way it was in Paris twenty years ago. So we drove to the new suburb close by called "Satellite City," where modern houses, some maintaining the strange Dutch roofs, and new apartment houses were rising on broad, newly landscaped streets. Near here we

Dutch roofs and modern houses

Brown nets drying by the Java Sea

dined in a restaurant on the famous Rijsttafel dishes which, in the original ceremony, consisted of one hundred separately served dishes, but still are delicious fare when taken in small part. All along the roads was a continuous market, still open at twelve o'clock. The flickering lights of the food stalls burn half the night in Jakarta, and everything is sold—from vegetables to furniture.

We drove back across the city to Chinatown. As we passed within four blocks of the Des Indes Hotel along a street overhung with trees, a rare street lamp shed a timid ray of light along a row of small, white buildings, and in large letters I saw a familiar name: Soedarpo Corp. We stopped suddenly and here—four blocks from the hotel which could find no trace of them—were my friends' office buildings. We scribbled a note and left it under the door.

In the old part of the city fires glowed from the street braziers on which fragrant, spicy food was cooking. We ate bowls of freshly cut sweet apples and tangerines, wandered among the flower stands and stalls along little passageways that were as alive as State Street at the rush hour. It was soon two A.M. and we were drinking a last coffee at a stand.

The next day I stopped in the little shop to see my friend and have another look at the black sapphire just as Soedarpo Sastrosatomos came bouncing into the lobby, looking very handsome, all in white linen. We hurried off in a little MG for his lovely home among palm trees and flowers on a tree-lined street just three blocks from where my friends of the gem shop lived. Soedarpo's beautiful wife, Minarsih, was wearing Western dress, and one of their lovely children was wearing an American cowboy costume, complete to boots.

After a lunch consisting of seventeen different dishes we piled into an American sedan and drove through the hills of Java to Borgo, where there are lovely homes and the summer palace.

Along the way, banana trees shaded the hillsides and coconut palms rose in the valleys sheltering little houses swathed in bougainvillaea. It grows cooler in the rising hills, and the island lies green and moist.

We returned by way of the old city of Jakarta, where shipping pours through the harbor to and from the world.

Doors to the treasure of the Pacific

An empty bowl

Ancient export houses with crudely carved, weather-bleached doors and the old museum look out on a lazy square.

Fishermen's nets are spread along one side of the harbor, and in a doorway of a banana-leaf hut a child sits on a dirt floor, just having emptied his bowl of rice. On the roof is a flat grass tray of coconut (copra) and fish drying in the sun.

The next evening Minarsih wore a beautiful sarong, with a cummerbund and a lace top (a kabaya), and delicate Indonesian jewelry. She looked like a delicately tinted figurine. We dined and talked of the days when the Sastrosatomoses lived in Washington D.C., and I was with *Harper's Bazaar,* and of our mutual friend Lotti. They told me of the other islands which I had lost too much time to visit this time. I left in the middle of the night for Singapore.

On the plane I opened the tiny box in my purse that contained the black sapphire which I had finally purchased, and in the box with it was a small engraved silver pillbox—a gift from the Kusumobrotos. The star in the sapphire was dancing brightly over the stone.

Hong Kong

DOORWAYS OF THE JEWELED HARBOR

A SILVER WIRE flashes in the moonlight. Another glistens above and below it as the barbed-wire fence stretches over the low moonlit hills, across dusty gray ditches and along the wet rice fields. Lost momentarily behind a clump of bushes and in the shadows under the trees, the shining wires rise again from the tall grass, traced by the light of the moon; appearing and disappearing, running relays from fence post to fence post, touching and hurrying on connecting with cement road blocks giving way to the silver Shum Chun River that marks the bamboo curtain across the Kowloon Peninsula from Deep Bay to Mirs Bay.

The wire halts for the white highway and the shining steel rails of the Kowloon–Canton Express, where two men with guns briefly take the place of the wire.

Beyond the barbed wire is Red China. On this side of it, the hills of Kowloon (British Crown Colony of Hong Kong) cast deep shadows over the rice fields.

Villages lie blanched in the light of the moon, and the wet rice paddies scatter over the flat land like bits of broken glass. A dusty country market lies along a tree-lined lane that drops away from the highway in a black-and-white patchwork of shadow and moonlight.

The overhanging roofs of the market stalls touch and form a cover over the market. It's late, and only a few figures huddle around the shops and stalls in the flickering of the kerosene lanterns. Enormous white pigs branded with yellow paint squeal in basket cages. A narrow dirt path zigzags between the covered bins of tea, spices, dried fish, and shelves of heavy pottery. Most shelves are bare, but tomorrow they will be stacked and running over with vegetables, rice, fruit, and melons that grow in the little valleys around the market of Sheungshui, not far from the Red border.

Toward Hong Kong Harbor, the clay hills build up around Shatin Heights outside the town of Kowloon, and below are acres of cement-block refugee houses rising layer on layer, crowded together in the valley. The moonlight turns the mass of cement into a gray mountain and fills the hundreds of doors with black shadows. These are doors to a new life for millions of refugees who cross the barbed wire from Red China. Hundreds more of the block houses rise on the acres leased from Red China known as the "New Territories."

In Kowloon the lights are out along Nathan Road, the shopping heaven of Hong Kong. The big signs can be read in the white night: Jewelry—Rattan Furniture—Watches—Cameras—Silks—Ivory—Shoes—Tailor—and so on until the shops step back into the shadow of the arcade that ends at Hong Kong Harbor, where the tired, if not old, Peninsula Hotel slouches along the bank of the bay.

It's here that the Star Ferry connects Kowloon Peninsula with the island of Hong Kong, and it's from here that Hong Kong Island takes captive all who behold "the Rock," inlaid with millions of jewels from its peak down to the black waters of the harbor: red, blue, white, green lights gleaming in a jeweled medallion that obliterates the stars, minimizes the moon, which turns its pale, envious face on the junks, the gala, lighted ocean liners, black freighters, and barges that lie among the less brilliant reflections of the lights of the city of Victoria that scatters its jewels over "the Rock."

The colored lights trail along the harbor and fade away. Others twist over the mountainside like necklaces, drifting away toward Repulse Bay on the other side of the towering rock, where the night is white and the sea, more moonlight than water, goes on forever. And the rock cliffs of the island drop down to the water in little coves or drift into big bays and sandy beaches: Deep Water Bay; Telegraph Bay; Repulse Bay; Stanley Bay; and Big Waterfall Bay, where a deep gash cuts into the island. In this sheltering harbor lies Aberdeen, the village of thousands of Chinese junks, wallowing in the mud and shallow water like black, half-open shells piled up by the tide. The thousands of masts rise in the face of the moon like a forest of black sticks. Half of the bay is black with the junks. Along the other shore the seafood showboats are lighted like enormous jukeboxes inlaid with tile, painted, their neon lights turning the water around them into the same gaudy pattern.

With the coming of the day the curtained doorways of the junks are thrown back, and life swarms over the catwalks and runways as it does over a city street. Weddings, celebrations, sorrows, and births take place on the bobbing junks nudging, bumping, rocking in the mud.

Thousands of families live, fish, work, and multiply on the junks of Aberdeen, many of them proud descendants of the feared Chinese pirates who roamed the China Seas.

The never-completely-stifled desire of man to set his home apart has brought strange things to the doorways of the junks to make them different, pretty, and comfortable.

Although many of the drawn curtains reveal only hungry children, empty rice bowls, and ragged mats, in one a mirror reflects a velvety red dahlia in a water glass beside a noisily ticking modern clock. Other treasures are glimpsed—a vacuum bottle, a doll, a framed photograph, an oil lamp on a shelf against a Persian-print curtain; a fresh, flowered pillow lies on a neatly-folded blue blanket; a flowered pot de chambre stands by the doorway on the front deck.

A young Chinese woman with prized gold teeth and a baby tied on her back in a square of red-checked cotton

A red dahlia and drying fish

washes two flowered cups and puts them carefully upside down on the shelf beside the red dahlia. Her hands stacked with wet clothes she has wrung from a flowered washbowl, she walks the long catwalk to hang them on a line strung from a platform on stilts above the black mud. Big, oval fish dry in the sun on more platforms along the bank.

Among the junks, occasional houseboats are hung with double fringes of shark fins, one of the island's big exports, drying on the railings of the flat tops. More fish lie in meticulous rows, like diamond shingles on the flat roofs.

Women in full-legged pants and coolie coats carry jugs of water and food back to the junks. An old man dozes in a rattan chair; a little girl brushes her hair with a scarred silver brush; a woman washes pale-green cabbage in a blue bowl; a baby is fed rice with chopsticks, by an ancient woman; a family huddles around a bowl of rice.

Along the edge of the black crust of junks, one breaks off here, another there, then another one, with their big wing sails spread, moving out to sea for fish.

Gliding among the junks, sampans pass back and forth to the floating neon palaces across the bay, where you choose your dinner over the rail from fish hanging in big nets in the water, cavorting in their cages.

As Aberdeen gets its fish from the fishermen of the Aberdeen junks, it turns its face the other way to the farmers of Shoushon Hill for fresh vegetables. Fields of pale green cabbage grow right to the doorways of the little houses. Covered with flowering vines, the roofs and chimneys have lost their shape and become domes of green leaves, lavender, purple, and blue flowers turning the little houses into Hänsel and Gretel fairy-tale houses against the black rock hills.

Beyond the cabbages of Shoushon Hill, the old yellow stone Repulse Bay Hotel looks out over the water from behind rows of potted marguerites, hydrangeas, purple petunias, sweet william, and swags of bougainvillaea where its broad veranda tables are set for lunch.

In the hills around the little Chinese market at Stanley are lovely villas and new houses, glimpsed through the trees. Approached through hillside drives, they are hidden among flowers and gardens. Overlooking Stanley Bay, is my friend Daphne's family's villa, its porches and terraces high above the sea. Its beach lies below, at the bottom of the two-way stone stairs that are edged with hundreds of potted plants. Hong Kong, like Spain, is a land of potted plants, whole gardens of plants in pots, but never planted in the ground.

Daphne's name is Li Ying Kwok, and she has the impeccable kind of chic, beautiful hands and delicate figure that make smart Chinese women look like finely-carved figurines. Daphne's family is a large clan from Shanghai, now scattered over China, Hong Kong, Singapore, and what was once Indochina—and other parts of the world. Her father, one of the great cotton merchants of Shanghai, as was the custom, had many wives and many children. The family dining room in the villa overlooking the sea has twenty-four brocaded chairs at the long oval table, all of them usually filled.

Daphne's magic Chinese words or beautiful English did wonderful things for me in many places long before I reached Hong Kong. It was Daphne who found small jade opium lamps that make wonderful table lighters for one-fourth what I was going to pay for them, and bargained for beautiful fragments of gilded carvings in the Thieves' Market, which is 99.9 per cent junk and food. But for the rare prizes, it's worth the crowds and the fun, the flights of street stairways, and the being trampled. It's incomprehensible where the items could have been found and why they would have to be stolen (if they were): old teakettles without spouts; chairs without backs or legs or bottoms; shiny new pottery and figurines brazenly marked "antique"; crystal that is glass; and emeralds and rubies courtesy Coca-Cola bottling company; old machinery and iron that would supply Stankiewicz with material for a thousand lifetimes of sculpture. Here and there is a tiny white jade lamp or an exquisite gilt carving stripped from temples in Red China (against the law to bring out of Hong Kong); some old jewelry; a brass bowl; a piece of Chinese faïence; or a cloisonné box. But these finds are rare.

A girl reads a newspaper in front of a stall where a cup and bowl from which she just had rice and tea stand on

Hong Kong news

A family dinner in the Thieves' Market

barrels of spice and dried fish. In front of the next stall, a family of ten cooks and eats in the street. Cards are written with a bamboo brush by an old man sitting on a stool at a tiny table, and are hung on the wall of a building to dry. A shop is fringed with shark fins, dried fish and ducks, over bins of almonds and vegetables. The bazaar is so thick with Chinese eating, sleeping, smoking, bargaining, buying, that it takes time to move. The camera lens is always up someone's sleeve or in a child's hair when you click the shutter. Narrow, steeply slanting streets, scarcely passable, have kangaroo-legged tables down the center loaded with ready-made clothes on sale, like the basement aisle of a department store.

Happy Valley runs through the heart of Hong Kong, between a flower-covered cliff and a hill grayed with little houses that rise in steps up the ravines and balance on the overhanging rocks. Below lies the Happy Valley Jockey Club —green grass, flowers, a fast track, and a multicolored mass of people from every part of the world, crowding from the rail to the terrace of the restaurant and bar that overlook the track.

The crowd is a mass of color: Chinese men in silk coats; Indian women in brilliant saris; Sikhs in purple, red, and flowered turbans; women in print kabayas; Chinese dancing girls with rhinestones in their hair and sparkling on their spike heels; slim oriental girls in silk Chinese sheaths slit to their stocking tops; beautiful oriental women in Western dresses and slacks; Britishers in inevitable sleeveless cashmeres under their tweeds; Americans with raincoats over their arms; and Indian men in their smartly cut Indian jackets mill about the betting windows and surge to the rail when "They're off!" in Happy Valley.

By the time the last race is won, the shadow of the rock cliff has crossed the valley and is climbing up over the little houses on the other side. The colorful crowd that hugs the rail has lost its brilliant accents in the shadow. Then it's the rush hour at the Star Ferry.

A shoemaker works in the light of the doorway of a sidewalk shop. He works very fast with the crudest, simplest tools and turns out handmade shoes in a few days. At night he boards his doorway up with the planks that lean against the wall. The fine tailors and dressmakers are hidden away on little side streets and second-floor back-room shops.

It's cocktail time in the old Peninsula Hotel lobby, long known as the place you can, sooner or later, find anyone who is in the Orient. True, the big lobby narrows the search down considerably, but once in the lobby you have to take bearings and get out the compass again, even to locate a friend for an engagement. Northeast side or southwest corner? Behind which one of the big pillars will the search end and you find your "Dr. Livingstone" sipping an orange squash or a whisky soda?

You have to love the Peninsula Hotel to stay with it, for water is available only two hours in the morning and two in the late day. The exact hours when the heavenly miracle takes place I cannot recall. I do remember, however, that I could never hit it off with the water schedule. It was too late in the morning or too early in the evening to achieve a bath. If I hit the water schedule, the towels were missing.

But out my window every evening Hong Kong's jewel box was laid open and millions of dollars' worth of neon jewels were scattered over Victoria's peak and floating on the harbor, and I made do with the pitcher of water again.

Dinnertime, and the Star Ferry takes you back across the harbor to Hong Kong where Italian orchestras play their sweet, mad music; where chicly dressed Chinese dance the cha-cha at the Paramount Club; down an alleyway the Parisian Grill serves wonderful Continental food. There's a small Chinese restaurant where even bird's nest soup becomes delicious; another where Peking duck is at its best. Daphne knows which and where.

If you're lucky, Hong Kong is Chinese with an international coating; if not, it's vice versa.

There's a Catholic church were we saw a special museum collection of Chinese paintings. There's a Chinese restaurant where we went for lunch and ended up attending a Chinese wedding. There's the beautiful temple where we had tea in a secluded corner with a holy attendant. There are the Gardens of Eucliff with a swimming pool walled on one side with blossoming orange trumpet vines, the other side dropping straight down into the bay.

Anything may come to light anyplace in Hong Kong, where great riches are enjoyed without assurance beyond today, and poverty exists with hope for tomorrow.

Sidewalk shoemaker

Down an alleyway

Japan

DOUBLE-EXPOSURE DOORWAYS

IN THE pale, chilly January morning, a distant gray skyscraper is framed in the gateway of a Shinto shrine, like a double exposure from two worlds, both schizophrenic Japan: a world half ancient, half modern, part Oriental, part Western. The shiny new Tokyo tower, cradling an entire five-story building in its mesh of steel, rises above tiny frame houses and throws its long shadow across the moat of the haughty, plain Imperial Palace.

This is Tokyo, where *sumo* matches monopolize the TV, and baseballs are whammed in the streets; where John

Wayne stands three stories high with a smoking gun, and across the street the all-male Kabuki players in kimonos, wigs, and falsetto voices recite poetic words written a thousand years ago; where there's a stone stove in many kitchens and a TV on the other side of the paper wall, a feather duster in every car and an electric pillow on the *tatami* (grass-mat floor); where women in kimonos clip along on their wooden clogs beside men in Madison Avenue flannels and British cashmeres.

Paradoxical Japan, with its language so foreign that there isn't a clue for communication, becomes a series of strange, vivid impressions like mental slides. "No Smoking" and "Newsstand" signs are works of calligraphic art. Street signs, though unreadable, are exciting. The endless flat streets of frail wooden houses hit the eyes with new dimension; restaurant signs, a drawing of a fish or a saki bottle, are striking in design. Huge medallions of artificial flowers stand on easels

Newsstand sign—works of art

At every shop door, a Japanese lantern

. . . in congratulations

fifteen feet high, like fantasies, in congratulations before a new shop. The impressions go on at the vegetable stands: pyramids of tangerines; huge, foot-long white radishes; oblong strawberries; piles of seaweed, leaves, and fish; magenta-pink cabbages like big Disneyland roses. Glimpses along the street: beautiful young girls in bright, Balenciaga-cut coats, short black hair and white gloves strolling past the big hotels; bicycles stampeding the streets during the busy hours; neon spectaculars flashing red and blue, red and blue; Japanese lanterns—big, little, white, blue, red, yellow, green; old women sitting on their knees in train seats as they would on their *tatamis;* inside, *hibachis* (charcoal stoves) with tiny red coals alive in the warm ashes, and beautiful examples of *ikebana* (flower arrangements).

Tokyo penetrates the mind quickly with fragments of sound: the rattle of rickshas over the uneven stones; the sound of rain on the light wooden houses; the click of hurrying wooden clogs on the uneven pavement; the wailing notes of the samisen as its lament seeps through the walls of a teahouse; the soft-spoken "sank you"; the sharp sounds of "hi hi" (yes, yes) constantly repeated through every conversation; the staccato of the language drifting meaninglessly all

Huge lantern at a temple door

around (while you strain your ears for a familiar sound).

The sound record of the mind picks up the muffled moving noises of the crowds along the Ginza; the eternal noise of new building; the baby-like, staccato voice of a jazz singer trying to stretch out words into the wail of a torch song; the childlike giggle that ricochets from one Japanese to another.

Just as the sounds and look of Tokyo pile up fast, the smells and flavors of the city have been drifting into consciousness: the fragrance of steaming cups of tea as varied as the essences of Grasse; pastry in the shop windows smelling warm and sweet; the first cherry buds, as fragile as snowflakes; the smell of fish along the markets and the delicious taste of golden tempura, the tender, deep-fried shrimp; the taste of *nuoc-mam* that flavors everything; the smell of tangerines as they're peeled in the theater; the sweetness of the decorated candy, as if it were perfumed; the warm bouquet of saki in a china thimble, and the taste of it on a cold night while sitting on a cold *tatami;* and raw fish (for some, not for me).

The impressions of Japan, fast and vivid, without understandable personalities to hold them together, remain dimensionless, fleeting fragments. It's the people of Japan that lodge in one's mind and radiate the true impressions that cannot be seen, cannot be told, but must be felt to arrange the incongruous bits of Japan into a meaningful picture.

Through the personality and avant-garde painting of Toko Shinado came the first glimmering of the physical dimension of Japan. Her articulate calligraphic painting, striving to define space, measured for my mind the unique proportions of Japan. Called abstracts by some, "ink and paintings in space" by others, Toko Shinado's work has reached boldly beyond the art of calligraphy so familiar to the Japanese. Toko Shinado's art has been exhibited in Europe, South America, and the United States (at the Guggenheim and Modern Museums in New York).

Some of her paintings, continuing from one canvas to another, gave meaning to the use of space with which the Japanese create sand gardens in long furrows with a rock or a small green plant forming a new feeling of space in an area which had held another conception of space before. It made me look again at the trees patiently shaped by string and wood; and the waterfalls and miniature trees of a tiny garden so proportioned as to seem quite normal in size. Her paintings tied together the elusiveness of things I had seen quickly, and afterward the natural beauty of Japan

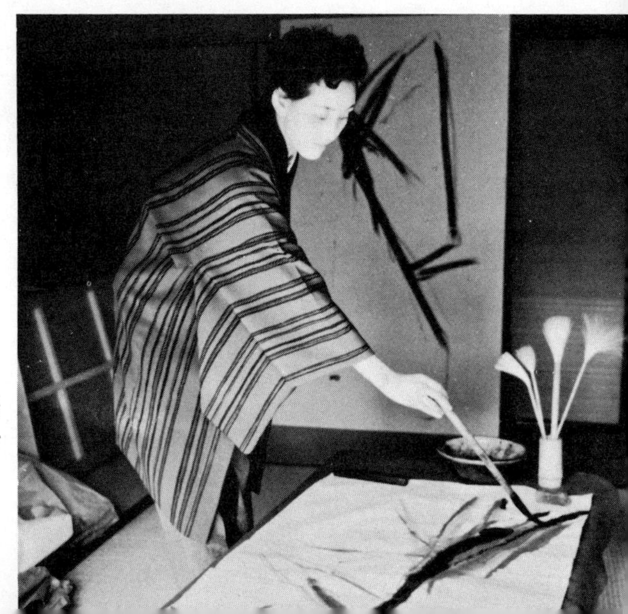

Gray and black ink on rice paper

seemed of a different dimension. The pine trees that grow like spikes up the pointed mountains, tipped quickly with snow, accent the sharpness of the ascent, and the land—I know now—is deep and sharp and staccato. The flat lakes somehow seem flatter than any other water. Orange trees dotted over the quickly changing levels of the land seem taller and thicker, cherry trees mass together for effect, and fig trees spread their silver net of limbs in small places in careful patterns.

More than her profound art, which I do not pretend to understand (but by which I do claim to be stimulated), Toko Shinado was to synthesize for me the many fragments of Japan, seemingly unrelated, that I had collected with my eyes and ears.

To be a guest in a Japanese home is rare, and I drove miles to Toko Shinado's house in a small suburb now swallowed up by the biggest city in the world. In the very old house with its lovely garden there was enough overlapping Eastern and Western in thought and feeling to give me swatches of the mixture and the pure, so that I could recognize gradations and match up some of my impressions of Japan.

There were the usual one-way slippers of varying sizes at the door, and the cold *tatami* mats. Mme. Shinado's living room had chairs and a low table, a beautiful antique *hibachi* (stove), also an electric heater, and a bookcase. My Japanese consisted of ten badly mangled words, and her English of about twenty faltering ones, but we talked a long time. We discussed books and magazines and fashions and other countries, and color. In her studio were stacks of paintings. We looked at many of them in various stages of completion, on thin paper that buckles with the ink that is applied with huge brushes, on a very low, flat table. The paper is stretched and mounted later. We had tea and talked about clothes, and she showed me many of her beautiful kimonos of fabrics she designed or painted. They were as different from the flowered kimonos of the Ginza as Mainbocher is from Macy's—stripes and small designs, mostly black or gray, or brown and white. Her dressmaker's name was the same as that of the dressmaker of the royal princess.

Mme. Shinado was extremely chic, with the figure of a *Vogue* model.

There was no chance to see a performance of the No (or Noh) drama, but a few days after I arrived I was sent a ticket to Kabuki by a young Japanese who had met me at the station in an official capacity. Attached was a note regretting he could not accompany me.

When I arrived at the Kabuki theater at four o'clock for the second and last five-hour performance of the day, the curtains were drawn back on the long, narrow stage, across which the players were grouped on pillows in magnificent kimonos and costumes. The scenery was realistic; the make-up was exaggerated. It was a lovely Japanese print with strange staccato sounds darting back and forth, punctuated with the singsong male falsetto of the heroine answering

Trees shaped with string

in a sad stanza of devotion and hovering doom. Then the staccato voices and stylized movements began to weave a mood of troubled love across the colorful stage. I was absorbed.

Suddenly I realized the seat next to me, on the aisle, was occupied, and I turned away from the stage to draw my coat in.

The gentleman said, "Good evening. Have you an English program?"

Kabuki among the tangerines

I said, "No," and he said, "I order one for you."

As he spoke in Japanese to the attendant, I observed he was a very handsome Japanese with slightly gray hair, cut in a rather undergraduate style, and he was wearing a dark gray suit that made him look very un-Japanese, but when he turned and looked straight at me with the program, I saw black triangular eyes and a classic Japanese face. He introduced himself in the soft oriental voice and said, "I'm sorry I'm so late," which sounded slightly like, "I'm thorry I'm tho late."

I was baffled, but said nothing except, "Yes, of course, not at all."

The stage grew very active and dramatic, and then the lights brightened and the charming man beside me smiled very slightly and said, "When San told me he had sent you a ticket, and you come alone because he must go back to school the day before he plan to, I told him you must not come to the opera alone. You might not understand—not enjoy. So I took the ticket. He tell you?"

I was extremely pleased to know I had a legitimate reason to claim this man as a friend and explained that San had failed to mention it.

"San's father and I are law partners, you know," he smiled, and this ended all explanations.

People continued to enter the theater with their string bags of tangerines, which they proceeded to peel and eat, dropping the peels on the floor. There was constant conversation and people eating bits of food from packages tied up in silk scarves. The Japanese gentleman asked if I understood Kabuki. I said I had seen the dancers but not the actual play.

He said, "Read the synopsis quickly and I tell you about it as it goes along."

He spoke with the slight Japanese difficulty over t, l, and v, although he had, I learned, spent several months in America and actually spoke English fluently. He was a devotee of the Kabuki. As the fair young maiden danced the exquisite fan dance, he explained, "He is seventy, grandfather of the small boy who performed in the preceding play as a dancer."

The grandfather was one of the famous players of feminine rolls and, incredible as it may seem, this rather stout man in elaborate kimono, speaking in a falsetto voice, created a heroine much more feminine, more believable than some of our leather-coated, deadpan actresses could ever hope to do. Kabuki is a family affair. Roles are passed from father to son for generations, and the players begin training at the age of seven.

The five plays that made up the evening of Kabuki were thrilling, and the off-stage sound effects and cues were very amusing. The audience came and went, ate, and shouted out their approval or praise in sharp outcrys.

Kiichi Itabahashi's quiet voice explained to me throughout the meaning of gestures, attitudes, and symbols that made the plays amusing and told the subtleties of the story.

The lion dance was partly performed on a runway through the audience, then continued on the stage. The tremendous amount and huge dimension of the costume was the maximum for one person to manipulate in a dance. The enormous mane flew about as the colossus of the Japanese theater charged and whirled. There were, of course, murders and ancient tricks from which some of our vaudeville acts must have sprung. There was suicide for lost love, and one play ended with the hair of the heroine's being shorn to signify she would remain a widow of the man who had just committed hara-kiri for honor, and never love again.

During the long intermission for dinner or refreshment in the theater restaurant, Mr. Itabahashi showed me the paintings of the famous actors in the halls of the theater and in precise, clipped English told me something of their famous roles and of the 1300 years of continuous dance in its various forms, from No to Kabuki, Bugaku, and the Bunraku (puppet theater).

The five hours passed quickly. By the time we left the crowded theater, crunching through the tangerine peelings, and went in search of tempura, the dinner hour was over and many of the restaurants were closed. We found one just closing, but they prepared the wonderful golden shrimp in batter with many side dishes of sauces and rice, and the

Eels and seafood

dinner ended with two huge strawberries, with green stems and leaves attached, served on a gray pottery plate with a pyramid of sugar to dip them in. We drank warm saki, next of kin to vodka.

As we walked back through the little streets to the Imperial, the Tokyo night was cool and quiet. An occasional ricksha passed by and the cli-ik, cli-ik of wooden clogs sounded in the shadows of the streets. The night clubs were ablaze with neon, and Japanese lanterns burned over doorways. We talked of many things in Japan, and Kiichi as I came to know him, asked eagerly about many things he had seen and enjoyed in America.

On the way to Imati and Hakani, the slides start again—orange trees bending with ripe fruit; cherry blossoms drifting like pink mist through the twisting streets of the little towns along the mountainous seashore; the staccato landscape turning quickly from peak to valley, from rock to sand along the sea that reaches to San Francisco. Phantom mountains push their tops through the silver mist, and serene above all is Mt. Fujiyama, the white-haired witch that centuries ago spat fire and lava over Japan.

Below the JAL plane from Tokyo to Osaka, Japan lays out her pictures of compact lakes and mountains. Below is the Nagara River, where the cormorant-fishing boats fish at night, with their fire reflecting on the water, and the sporting rapids of the Japanese Rhine, and the jagged seashore.

Along the road from big, busy Osaka to Kyoto, there's another Japan, a country of rice fields tucked into every small valley and lying at the foot of every hill, with the harvest of rice straw stacked in pagodas, pyramids, and cones, around poles and trees, and tied into strange shapes.

Finally Japan reveals the strangely beautiful city of Kyoto, which was for ten centuries the capital of Japan, lying in the flowering valley between green pine hills and the peak of Mt. Hiei.

And the slides continue:

Rows of gray frame houses and wide streets spin like a spider's web across the valley. Big resort hotels look down from pines and red wooden shrines and temples break the gray web of frame houses. Sand, flower, and rock gardens stretch and maneuver space; wood is piled in beautiful designs along the road. The summer palace, with its seven secluded teahouses among moss gardens, winding paths, gentle lagoons, and quiet streams gliding under arched bridges; the Emperor's library, with exquisitely painted silk walls and fabulous cabinet inlaid with thirty-seven different woods. Long streamers of colored silk rippling in the Kamo River, looped around pegs in the shallow water where men tramp the Yuzen-Zome dyed silks in the cold water, the secret of the brilliant, color-fast silk. The long strips of cloth hang from oversize clotheslines along the rocky banks and lie like flower beds in neat rows of pink, red, yellow, and orange on the grass. In dimly lighted rooms down small streets, old men sit at antiquated looms, weaving fabulous obi brocades of dozens of colored silk threads and strands of gold and silver, their hands throwing the shuttle back and forth so fast the eye loses it in its flight among the taut threads, weaving one yard a week of the precious cloth.

A country of rice fields

Rows of gray frame houses

In a public bath men, women, and children, covered with soapy lather, bathe in the small hot-water pool, like round-faced cherubs in a cloud. At the doorway a huge tree lends its trunk to a small Buddhist shrine that leans against it and repays the help with paper offerings shed over the tree's branches.

It was knowing Eiko, the young Japanese career girl, that made order out of my Kyoto impression slides. It was a cool evening, and we had seen the thousand and one gilded images of the thousand-armed goddess Kwannon in Kinkakuji Temple. We had visited the Heian shrine and talked with the holy maidens and priests; we had shopped and talked to the matmaker in his doorway; and had dined on dozens of tidbits of fish, eggs, rice, and beans, served in the beautiful crescent dish (bowls and teacup each of a different design), proving again the old saying, "Japanese food is eaten with the eyes." We walked down the main street where red, blue, green, white, and yellow lanterns were lighted and

Holy maidens

A huge tree shelters a small shrine

The matmaker

the small *pachinko* halls that open onto the street were crowded. I didn't realize *pachinko* was a pinball machine until I had my basket of silver marbles and we were pushing our way to the machine with the shortest line in front of it. I pulled the handle, and the silver marbles kept piling up in the trough along the front of the garish machine. In a few moments my basket and my hands were full of the metal balls, which we cashed in for cigarettes and walked along the strange street on the almost cold evening.

We walked far down the main street past doll shops, lacquer, kimono, and jewelry shops, and more *pachinko* halls spilling out into the street. We ate fresh pastry still warm and fragrant, and I took a cab back to my hotel. I rolled myself into my Japanese bedroll on the cool *tatami* and looked out the partly open door onto a Japanese garden.

The next day was cold and rainy. On the outskirts of Kyoto we entered the unique house of Japan's famous pottery designer, Kanjiro Kawai. The room beyond the mat-covered, raised vestibule was crowded with furniture of dark wood. On one side of the room were a *hibachi* and several small chairs. Kanjiro Kawai's famous carved masks (many of them humorous) were on the wall.

Mr. Kawai talked excitedly in Japanese to other people around the table as we had tea, and also to me. His son and friend Eiko translated as fast as they could, but the two of them could scarcely keep up. It was a lively tea.

In the courtyard were his kilns, with hundreds of designs and shapes in the making. Kawai had traveled in Europe and his son had studied in America, bringing back to the small studio off the courtyard Navajo rugs, Indian pottery, and other Americana.

In Kyoto, home of the famous Gion Geishas, we met Kofumi, a young *maika* (apprentice geisha) who is probably the most photographed girl in Japan, symbolizing Kyoto on travel folders and covers of magazines. She wore the paste-white make-up, and her black hair was oiled and stiffened into the elaborate hairdo of tradition. Shiny, crimson-red lip lacquer was applied to her lower lip only, and her eyes were outlined with black pencil. In her tiny room, where she knelt on the *tatami* before a miniature dressing table, were over twenty boxes of hair ornaments and shelves of expensive, exquisite kimonos. She laughed spontaneously and often, and giggled less than most Japanese. It takes her four hours to dress for a party or reception, which she attends almost every evening as an entertainer and hostess. Her two pony-tailed apprentices, aged nine and eleven, wore pleated skirts, sweaters, and looked like any American schoolgirls. They help her dress, and run her errands, and learn to dance the

Geisha: four hours to dress

delicate, suggestive classic dances, and play the three-stringed samisen, twanged to the accompaniment of gentle love songs.

The wide gold and silver brocade obi was wound around Kofumi, then secured, and the ends arranged down the back in panels to the floor. Another beautifully kimonoed young *maika* appeared and she and Kofumi stuck their *tabis* into the T-straps of their *kopis* (eight-inch-high wooden clogs), bowed and said good-by, and clicked out into the stone street where a ricksha took them, chattering, away to a big reception.

We crossed the street to the teahouse of the Gion Geisha school, where a tea master was teaching the intricate art of the ceremony to young *maikas*. This gentleman was the sixteenth descendant of the originator of the tea ceremony. He sat on his knees and demonstrated with his fan—the most articulate thing in the world in the hands of a Japanese who knows the art of using it. The details of the ceremony take years to perfect but, briefly, the ritual lasts about a half hour and all participating must know the art. Each movement has meaning as the tea is whipped to a fragrant, green foam. To drink from the handleless teacup before turning it the proper number of times or with the design of the cup in the wrong position is as gauche as eating pie with a spoon. The slow, tranquil movement of the hands during the ceremony is absolute poetry. The ceremony is related to the season and this theme is carried out from the color of the teacakes to the flower arrangement and scrolls in the alcove. The purpose of the ritual is to relax and meditate, to invite peace and happiness—not to gulp and gab.

My last evening in Kyoto I was invited to the home of a young Kyoto kimono merchant.

Their house was completely Japanese: stone stove in the kitchen and shelves (kimono closets) in the bedrooms, where bedrolls are put down at night—no other furniture except scrolls and vases of flowers, except in one room where the only item was a large television set about which we all laughed. These uncluttered houses, from the kimono merchant's to the summer palace, had finally taken effect and I realized that I actually lived like Langley Collyer. What did I need with all the things that bulge the doors of my closets—things I never use: the bric-a-brac that covers my tables and my shelves; the many chairs; the rugs; the curtains; the lamps; the candlesticks; the pictures and mirrors; the old suitcases and worn-out handbags; heelless shoes and outdated clothes; the dresses with hems too long or too short; fabrics unmade; old typewriters; broken china and nicked crystal . . . It made me weary to think of it as I sat there on the cool *tatami* with warm tea and enthusiastic, thoughtful people with clear minds and uncluttered lives.

I was back in Tokyo and the time had come to leave Japan. As I waited in the little alcove near the main entrance of the old Imperial where Kiichi was meeting me to see me off to the airport, I couldn't help thinking that this long-touted, quakeproof old hotel could only really be the *result* of a severe earthquake. This structure could not have been designed and built. It must surely have been shaken down into the distorted, elegant mass of contradictory pillars, beams, projections, and confusion of stone and brick.

Exploring the old hotel is almost as adventurous as exploring the lost temples of Angkor, as romantic as the castles in Spain; and its lush interior of bizarre elegance is like a tour through the Seraglio. The many pillars of lava rock and brick that hold up its low ceilings have no particular order, and its maze of corridors and passages are constantly changing course and levels: up two steps and down a slanting hall, turning to the right, jogging to the left, with dead ends. Its miles of deep scarlet carpet may end in a broom closet. A plush-curtained doorway leads up a small stone back stairway.

The walls ignore right angles and are the same inside as out—huge, thick brick walls and pillars sans plaster, though sometimes with touches of gilt. Stone stairs zigzag through the maze and may end perfunctorily at the door of the ladies' room. There are many entrances to every room, and the arcade is a shopping delight if you mark the walls with chalk to find your way out. Small bars and tea rooms look out on small courtyard gardens where streams of water, rocks, and trees and flowers form a lovely formal garden. There are no windows from the public rooms to the streets. It took so long to find one of the restaurants on one evening that the dinner hour was over when we got there.

Somewhere, surely, there's a hidden well of tears of those who made rendezvous at the old Imperial and were never able to find one another. The halls must be haunted with the spirit of the lovely young girl and the boy who met in the red-carpeted hall, spoke, and fell deeply in love, promising to meet the next day in the same sheltered alcove. The boy found his way and returned, waited and waited, and then went disconsolately away. The girl returned day after day to search through the hallways, but they never met again.

There must be, somewhere in this great pile of stone and plush, a tinge of regret for those who lost their way to the entrance and missed their planes and trains. There are, I can imagine, people still wandering about who came to stay only a few days.

The tiny, diamondback music-master chairs huddle like giggly young girls around monstrous settees with two-story backs that stiffly enclose a whole visiting Japanese family.

As the unhurried Tokyo evening falls, the old dowager Imperial, in red velvet and gilt, with great pomp is hostess to elegant Japanese functions. Big chauffeured cars deposit many men in striped trousers and cutaways at the doors.

Young *maikas* in beautiful and costly gold-and-silver-embroidered kimonos, with snow-white faces and elaborate hairdresses, arrive by twos graciously receiving the guests as entertainers and hostesses.

The old hotel looks snobbishly at the slim, tall, new ten-story Imperial that keeps in touch by a breezeway hall from the second floors across the old back entrance, where men carrying briefcases and tourists loaded with luggage swarm in and out.

As I mused the time went by, and I suddenly realized it was past time for Kiichi and I would miss my plane if I waited another moment. I summoned a porter and grabbed my hand luggage. At the same time Kiichi emerged from the deep interior of the old hotel with a strange look on his usually serene face, and his English was part Japanese.

"I not been in hotel for long time—I be damn if I find this place."

He stopped and looked at me seriously, and his black eyes flashed with incredulity.

We ran for the cab.

Hotel Imperial: was there an earthquake?

Hawaii

DOORWAY TO THE ONLY AMERICAN THRONE

THROUGH the doorway of the last and only American Royal Palace, polished black walnut and French crystal chandeliers gleam and the throne room is hushed with red velvet and gilt. Less than seventy years ago the last of the Hawaiian kings sat on the rich brocade-velvet throne in Iolani Palace in Honolulu. Outside, the soft trade winds stirred the palms and the Pacific caressed the white sands. Here King Kalakaua, the "merry monarch," held his last court in royal feather capes. Only royalty could wear feathers and only the royal catamarans could traverse the beautiful lakes and rivers.

Then the gentle paradise island passed under the rule of Liliuokalani, the first and last queen of the Islands, and on into the hands of revolutionaries who imprisoned the flamboyant queen for nine months in a chamber at the top of the black stairs. The queen's court sparkled for a brief two years with jewels from America and gowns from Europe. English-tailored uniforms mingled with the feathers and the fun. Then the fine feathers, costly carriages, jewels, and silks that had come to the Islands from the outside world were put aside and the poetic islands' history was from then on written in prose and punctuated with hard currency and progress.

The old palace is still known as Iolani Palace, which means "Bird of Heaven." Feather kahilis, the symbol of royalty, line the walls of the throne room, some of them reaching to the ceiling, the soft feather drums moving gently in the breeze from the big windows that open onto the piazza. Older kahilis (in the Bishop Museum) stand on poles of human shin bones joined together like bamboo.

Sometimes a slim, dark woman moves gracefully about the halls and porticos of the palace in a white cotton dress with a slight train and a red-patterned kerchief around the neck, which was once the formal Hawaiian dress. Her name is Iolani, too, and she is the keeper of the throne room. But much more than that—in Iolani's graceful body and expressive hands lives the memory of the traditional hula and ceremonial dances of the old Polynesian Hawaii, the folk dances of the last island civilization. She alone knows some of the dances now extinct. Children were once trained in the perfection of the dance (as in the European ballet), beginning at the age of seven, but this is no more. Following the Mother Hubbard, brought to the islands by the missionaries, came the tourists, the fox trot, and the waltz; and the hula became do-it-yourself night-club entertainment.

A mischievous sense of humor keeps the Hawaiians (mixture of seven races) singing and dancing, laughing like children, even when they are sad. They are still as enigmatic as their Polynesian ancestors who came in catamarans across the South Pacific and lived on the beautiful islands splashed with jasmine-pink hibiscus and purple bougainvillaea; playing on the velvet beaches; living on dates, coconuts, bananas; living in fear of Pele, goddess of the great Mauna Loa, mountain of fire, brimming over with boiling red lava. Sometimes they appeased the angry goddess with sacrifices of their own blood, and the sea gods demanded strange things of them in exchange for fish. The *menehunes* (pixies) were always at work in the jungles, the misty valleys, and the sugar cane. The hill of Kauai, the sleeping giant, was filled with the red fire that might belch from his mouth if he were angered. But there was always cool shade under the big monkey-pod trees, and the sandalwood trees were sweet and soft, to be carved into images of those gods and goddesses the Polynesians feared and those who protected them. Worshipping the natural rocks and stones that suggested forms of animals, fish, or birds made the natives feel safe and happy. They danced the hula on the white beaches, speaking with their hands and singing the stories of their daily paradise. And these are the dances that Iolani knows; this *was* Hawaii.

But the capricious winds of the South Pacific brought warring tribes, invaders, friends, and strangers to the islands: British, Russians, Americans, bringing with them cattle, horses, missionaries, and the calico *muu-muu* (Mother

Hubbard) to cover the natives' bronze bodies instead of their grass skirt and *malos.*

The superstitions and myths of the old Hawaii still exist in the hearts of many of the people, and moonlit glades and shady rock coves are still haunted by spirits.

And Hina, the mother of all the Hawaiian gods, stands on a rock altar along the sea on Alice Kamokila Campbell's estate. And wasn't I told that this huge, strangely shaped stone was found buried in the sand on the beach after Pearl Harbor by Kamokila's retainer, who was struck immovable on the spot? And the massive stone goddess was moved up the beach onto its rock pedestal by strange music and the gentle touch of a child's hand.

Tucked away in private gardens there are crude wood carvings, and the misty Mauna Loa still holds a strange, hypnotic attention over the islands, drawing the sound of the sea and turning the wings of the birds and the faces of the flowers toward her.

It is said that all of old Hawaii that remains is five things: the *luau,* the Hawaiian feast; the twelve-letter alphabet, where every word ends in a vowel, consonants are always separated by a vowel, and every vowel is pronounced, even if there are three together; surfboarding, which was once the sport of island kings; the hula, in a popular version; and

Hina, mother of all Hawaiian gods

Vitamin-fed pineapples on the hilltops

the exotic flower-islands themselves, beautiful beyond belief. The rest of old Hawaii is in the Bishop Museum.

The world of the Happy Kings has passed into oblivion, leaving behind scarcely a relic or a ruin to tell the story. The missionaries burned their beautiful pagan carvings; their feather finery was outlawed and the royal sea bird became extinct—40,000 of these small birds gave their feathers for one supple, silky cape for the giant Hawaiian kings. The great sandalwood trees that perfumed the air have disappeared.

The new Hawaii, U.S.A., is an island of luxurious hotels, strung cabaña to cabaña along the sands of Waikiki. A richer-than-Fifth-Avenue array of shops lines the streets of Honolulu. Jaguars, MGs, Buicks, and Cadillacs prowl the curving roads that edge the sea; brassy bands alternate with too-polished Hawaiian performers in posh night clubs; used-car lots with pennants flying and Pepsi-Cola palaces squeeze in among the stately palms. The only grass huts are the posh ones on the beach. Diamond Head, so called because English sailors thought, upon finding shining rock crystal, they had found diamonds, now sparkles with diamonds from Tiffany's.

Islands fringed with beaches

The islands of Hawaii are like a row of cookies stamped out in different shapes, with lacy, white-doily edges of sand, served up on a blue plate and doused with sunshine—all of the same volcanic rock, all mountainous, all with hidden waterfalls, jungle growth, and flowers. One island "the man named Dole" made famous for pineapples; another "the Bostonian named Parker" made famous for cattle. When the sugar-cane tassels and harvest time comes the fast fires burning off the dry leaves blaze over all the islands, leaving the juicy, sugar-filled stalks to be harvested. And the little, patched-together houses of the tara farmers, surrounded by their scraggly fields, dot every island. The pineapple fields climb high up the mountain to keep out of the way of the sugar planters, and the millions of acres of pineapples that have brought wealth and good living to Hawaii are a miracle of artificial growing and pollenization. The soil is so poor that the growers say they merely prop the plants up in the soil while they feed them on vitamins and iron. If pollenated by Nature's hummingbird method, the big, delicious pineapples would be cluttered up with seed. But there are no hummingbirds in Hawaii, so science does the job seedlessly.

Far below the green pineapple fields the ocean weaves a lacy edge of blue around the island of Oahu. In Chinn Ho's hibiscus-pink car we zoom along the road above Pearl Harbor past patches of water cress, along roads narrowed with sugar cane on both sides, along the sea.

Chinn Ho, this slight man in scholarly glasses and crew haircut with a rich, quiet humor and an inevitable cigar, was graceful with his time, taking many people, as he did me, to see some of the old Hawaii, which he carefully preserves and restores as he helps build the new Hawaii. Every tree is important, and his builders have to account for one that is missing when Chinn Ho has marked it to stay. Among his vast activities that reach far beyond the islands Chinn Ho builds beautiful, ultra-modern houses on the sloping hills around Honolulu looking out over the Pacific, with flower gardens and lagoons stocked with pink flamingoes, and banana trees at their backs.

The car turns away slowly, up a ravine through a fenced lane that grows narrower and narrower; the big car noses through the overhanging trees and spreading bushes where wild peacocks glint through the undergrowth. Many gates have to be opened and closed as Chinn Ho's cattle drift in bunches over his valley ranch.

Tara farms dot the island

Pepsi-Cola among the palms

Diamond Head—sparkling with diamonds from Tiffany's

The lane ends in a clearing where smoke rises along a rocky cliff and spirals above a grove of trees. The car comes to a halt and we start up the rocky path. As we near the men working among the piles of stones in the burning bush, an outline takes shape and the crumbling, broken walls of a huge sacrificial temple appear in the thick overgrowth. One large room is outlined with a high wall. Above it, on higher ground in another walled area, is where the altar stood between two small trees. Along the two rooms of the temple are stalls for the sacrificial stock and a small room where priests slew the animals. Another large stone is shaped for human sacrifice. The woods had concealed the sacrificial temple for many years, scattering its walls and hiding its secrets. In the thick woods around it once stood the thatched-roofed houses of the village.

Chinn Ho could never quite understand why everyone wants to see his cows when there are so many other beautiful things to see. But if you do, you may. One magazine wanted to photograph him with his cows and he obliged—with cigar, of course.

We pass the wild big bay where the surfboarding is best and most adventurous, and where the last king of Hawaii, who was an enormous man, maneuvered a fifteen-foot surfboard.

"Here the road should be moved back," explains Chinn Ho, "it is blocking the sea and changing the shoreline, which will eventually wash the sand away and destroy the beach."

Chinn Ho *is* Hawaii on the move. His father came to the islands many years ago from China, eighty days across the Pacific, over which I had just flown in a Pan American Jet Clipper in eleven hours.

Back in my room at the Halekulani Hotel, with the doors open onto my balcony, I can feel the sweet, salty spray as the tide swooshes upon Waikiki Beach and leaves it like ivory velvet. The tide has removed every footprint and wiped the slate clean for another day.

The tide swooshes upon Waikiki Beach

And the great hotels that made my travels a pleasure: most with a view worthy of the View Finders' Club—

London—The Dorchester—On Park Lane overlooking Hyde Park

Amsterdam—The Amstel—On the banks of the Grand Canal

Lisbon—Estoril Palace (30 minutes by car from Lisbon)—Facing the Esplanade

Madrid—The Wellington—With a wonderful viewpoint

Paris—The Meurice—Along the Gardens of the Tuileries

Rome—The Flora—At the top of Via Venéto

Athens—The Grande Bretagne—On Constitution Square

Istanbul—Istanbul Hilton—Overlooking the Bosporus and the Golden Horn

Cairo—Nile Hilton—On the banks of the Nile

Beirut—The Commodore—New and neat (no view)

Delhi—The Oberoi Imperial—Center of everything

Kathmandu—The Royal—Bewitching old palace

Banaras—Clarks—Not far from the Ganges (everything but a view)

Agra—Clarks—The only place

Calcutta—The Oberoi Grand—On famous Chowringhee Road

Bangkok—Arawan—At the edge of the city

Phnom Penh (*Cambodia*)—Le Royale—Filled with atmosphere and old elegance

Saigon—The Majestic—At the banks of the Saigon River

Singapore—Raffles—The heart of Singapore

Jakarta—(Lucky if you have friends)

Hong Kong—Peninsula—On Hong Kong Harbor

Tokyo—The Imperial—The magnificent maze

Honolulu—The Halekulani—On the sands of Waikiki